MW00683118

GROUNDWORK GUIDES

Series Editor
Jane Springer

GROUNDWORK GUIDES

The News
Peter Steven

Groundwood Books
House of Anansi Press

Toronto Berkeley

Groundwood Books / House of Anansi Press
110 Spadina Avenue, Suite 801, Toronto, Ontario M5V 2K4
or c/o Publishers Group West
1700 Fourth Street, Berkeley, CA 94710

We acknowledge for their financial support of our publishing program the Canada
Council for the Arts, the Government of Canada through the Canada Book Fund
(CBF) and the Ontario Arts Council.

Library and Archives Canada Cataloguing in Publication
Steven, Peter
The news / Peter Steven.
(Groundwork guides)
Includes index.
ISBN 978-0-88899-822-4 (bound).—ISBN 978-0-88899-823-1 (pbk.)
1. Press–Influence. 2. Reporters and reporting. 3. Freedom of the press. 4. Prejudices in
the press. 5. Press monopolies. 6. Press–Asia. I. Title. II. Series: Groundwork guides
PN4731.S843 2010   070.4'3   C2009-906508-8

Design by Michael Solomon
Typesetting by Sari Naworynski
Index by Lloyd Davis

Groundwood Books is committed to protecting our natural environment. As part
of our efforts, this book is printed on paper that contains 100% post-consumer
recycled fibers, is acid-free and is processed chlorine-free.

Printed and bound in Canada

Contents

To the courageous journalists around the world
who lost their lives in the past year.

Chapter 1
News Is Power

> We, unintentionally, are killing and wounding three or four times more people than the Vietcong do.... We are not maniacs and monsters, but our planes range the sky all day and all night, and our artillery is lavish and we have much more deadly stuff to kill with. The people are there on the ground, sometimes destroyed by accident, sometimes destroyed because Vietcong are reported to be among them. This is indeed a new kind of war.
> — Martha Gellhorn[1]

Martha Gellhorn was one of the best reporters of the twentieth century. As a prominent US journalist, she had covered the Spanish civil war of the 1930s, and the bombing of London and the liberation of the Nazi concentration camps during the Second World War. So in the summer of 1966, it was quite natural that she should apply for a press pass to report on the war raging in Vietnam. Within hours of her arrival in Saigon she had begun to write about the effects of the war on Vietnamese civilians.

What she witnessed shocked her. Her reports were raw, fierce and angry. They punctured the good image of the US military. Then came Gellhorn's second shock. None of the newspapers she regularly worked for in the US would print her stories. In the end only one small paper agreed, and then only after her reports had appeared in Britain. When she tried to return to Vietnam a few months later the US Army refused her a press pass.

Why Does It Matter?

Martha Gellhorn's experience reminds us of the crucial need for reliable information. How would you feel if your neighbor told you that SARS (Severe Acute Respiratory Syndrome) had broken out in the east end of the city, but you had no access to news media — no radio or TV, no newspapers, no Internet? You might get some information from a nearby hospital or from the police. But health workers and the police have their own jobs to do and can't be relied on to provide a well-balanced overview. Governments, schools, the military, religions, corporations and the courts all play a big role in shaping how we live our lives. But more than any of them the media have become the most powerful institutions in many societies today. Our information on almost everything comes through the media. Even if we ourselves become newsmakers or take part in significant events, we rely on the news media to report that to others. And it's not just about information. The media strongly influence the issues we think about, how we judge events, how we assess the past and how we act.

From the media we not only receive information and ideas on big issues such as wars, politics and the economy, we also take in messages about other people and other cultures. We absorb ideas about how to behave or about what is acceptable or unacceptable in our culture. Sometimes we become aware of these media influences. Frequently we do not. This obviously affects children as well — a crucial consideration in assessing images of war from Iraq, Afghanistan, Sri Lanka and the Democratic Republic of the Congo.

News people often tell us that free media provide the oxygen for a healthy democracy. Reliable news helps us maintain our civil rights — to speak openly, to gather with others in public, to vote and run for office. But free media also help maintain our basic human rights — to food, safety and health. Without the ability to receive and distribute basic news information we live in fear and danger — a long way from democracy. These principles have been agreed upon by most countries in the world through the United Nations treaties on human rights. Not only must citizens have the right to speak, write and express their views, they must also have the right to receive news and information from a wide variety of sources.[2]

In addition, the news matters because the organizations that gather and distribute news have become a major economic force in themselves. The news media employ millions of people, gobble up tremendous resources and receive countless benefits from governments. And through this economic power they attain political might as well. Some media owners stay in the business, even when they are losing money, precisely to maintain that political leverage.

Since the global crisis of capitalism in 2008, some news media organizations have gone out of business. In response, many commentators, especially in the US, from traditionalists to radicals such as Michael Moore, have worried that all newspapers are doomed. It is still unclear whether or not the news business as a whole has entered a major crisis. But the situation has underlined quite starkly the importance of high-quality news to democracy. I'll return to economic issues in later chapters.

Many people believe that they are immune to the bad influences of the media. "I grew up with it," they say. "I know when I'm hearing a biased report. I know the difference between the real world and the media world; I'm not affected." And yet, companies with billions of dollars to spend in psychological research and advertising disagree. They feel confident that the media can affect people in all sorts of ways, sometimes without our knowledge. That doesn't mean we're all dupes and zombies, brainwashed to behave uniformly and believe everything we see and hear. However, it does mean that we need defenses. We need tools to understand how the news media work. We also need the humility to recognize that we can be influenced in subtle and not-so-subtle ways.

Most of us don't want to live as hermits. Though many people spend their lives in a decidedly anti-social manner, most feel a need to be hip or at least up-to-date and reasonably well informed. We recognize that knowledge about the world brings us status, or at least prevents us from looking ignorant. The only way to acquire this knowledge is to "keep up with the news." But in this process of keeping up — by reading, watching, listening — we also get drawn into all sorts of social and cultural ideas and feelings. We don't simply scan the information; we are influenced and affected by it. Whether we like it or not, and whether we know it or not, we enter into a relationship with the news.

Most people don't have time to give the news media their undivided attention. In fact, most of us can absorb the news while carrying on another activity. Many listen to the radio at work or in their cars; others often catch the evening TV news while preparing dinner. Many only have time to skim their newspaper while gulping breakfast or wedged into a subway car. And millions of people share a newspaper at schools, libraries or work.

The news presents us with many different types of information. And because it always comes packaged in some form of narrative, or story, it always involves some elements of entertainment. Information and entertainment go hand-in-hand. You can't have one without the other. In fact, we could say that the news is never just news. It also represents people and groups. It presents an image of us, or people like us (i.e., in our social class,

Missing People

Women and News

Half the population, but only a fifth of the news is the conclusion drawn from three international studies of women in the news. Although more women journalists are active than ten years ago, women as the focus of stories remain a distressingly low 21 percent, even though they make up 50 percent of the population. And although women now outnumber men as TV presenters, or anchors, the studies reveal that women's images are used to sell the news — to adorn it rather than make it. Women may be photographed much more often than men, but most of these images come from items on entertainment and celebrity.[3]

Focus of news subjects:	Men 72%	Women 28%
Experts:	Men 83%	Women 17%
Victims:	Men 33%	Women 66%
Newspaper reporters:	Men 70%	Women 30%

News stories that discuss gender inequality: 4%

ethnic group or region). When many people read or watch or listen to the news they also wonder if a picture or story about someone like themselves will have an effect on them personally. Does the news validate me/us? Does the news denigrate me/us? Does the news ignore me/us?

An International Scope

North America and Western Europe are drowning in news media. There's so much that people often feel overwhelmed by information, opinion and chatter. But in many other parts of the world, people don't take

Canada's *National Post* newspaper published a splashy feature called "The Woman Issue" in 2007. The *Post* is based in Toronto, one of the most ethnically and racially diverse cities in the world. Yet fifty-nine of the sixty-one photos and illustrations in the section depicted white women.[4]

The representation of non-whites, including aboriginal people in North America, Australia and Aotearoa (New Zealand), continues to be largely negative, rife with examples of exoticism, trivializing and misrepresentation. For example, several major studies since the 1950s have shown the Aotearoa media to be consistently biased against Maori people. And in Canada the picture of Muslims is particularly loaded with stereotypes, says Shahina Siddiqui of the Council on American-Islamic Relations. The general image the news presents is that "Islam condones, encourages and recommends violence." And Muslim women are pictured as "suppressed, repressed, oppressed and depressed because of Islam. If only they would wear a miniskirt their woes would be over," Siddiqui says, describing the typical media view of Muslim women.[5]

news for granted. Many are starved for information or for accurate news of the most basic types. News about health conditions, political unrest, floods or other dangerous situations could mean the difference between life and death. Millions of people have no electricity and millions more cannot read. A wind-up radio or a local newspaper read aloud at school or work may be the best sort of news available. Others, in countries such as China and Iran, have plenty of news and high-tech machines to deliver it, but accuracy and a range of viewpoints may be entirely missing.

Different areas of the world get vastly different quantities of accurate, relatively unbiased news. Thus the meaning and importance of the news varies greatly across the world. Different types of news media dominate in different places. In North America most people get their news through television, while in Africa it's via radio. In countries where the government keeps a tight lid on TV most people rely on small newspapers and international radio for news they can trust, or at least use as a counterpoint. In addition, different types of media employ different news practices. For example, a newspaper story usually contains much greater detail than a TV story and somewhat more than the same item reported on radio. On the other hand, TV's use of pictures, sound and graphics can bring home a news story in a much more powerful way than text alone. Stories that deal with long-term trends, with the exception of some documentaries, usually fare poorly on TV and radio. In contrast, radio news can be much more immediate and is often less subject to editorial control.

Literacy rates, which vary widely across the world, also affect the news. Millions of people who cannot read rely solely on TV or radio. Even if they have access to newspapers and the Internet, their range of news is limited. And because newspapers generally carry more prestige than other media, people without literacy find themselves cut off from the news provided to elites and ruling classes.

Finally, competition to the main news sources and alternative sources of news depend greatly on the type of economic and political systems in place. In many capitalist countries media firms have been regulated to some extent by the government. That's because in a purely competitive system the strongest, biggest firms tend to push or buy out their rivals and citizens can only get their news from monopolies. But in other situations a weak or corrupt government has allowed or even stimulated monopolies to grow. To some degree this has taken place in the television industries of Brazil and Mexico (see Chapter 3).

News Concepts

Some basic concepts always crop up when people talk about the news media.

Professional journalism came into existence as a concept at the end of the nineteenth century. According to this set of beliefs, reporting is a discipline that must be learned. Like a doctor who takes an oath, journalists swear to be ethical, unbiased, objective and fair in their work. Amateurs, they argue, are incapable of this.

Neutrality is used by journalists to mean that they don't take sides when covering a story. If two people or two groups put forward two different positions, the journalist reports both, without favoring one or the other. Even the word "cover" suggests that the story exists on its own and that the reporter simply observes, then communicates it to readers.

Objectivity and unbiased reporting are phrases used by journalists to suggest that when they look into a situation or talk to people or follow events, they don't let their own views affect their reporting and writing. The reporter leaves her or his particular views about a subject out of the story.

The news media prides itself on providing facts. "Comment is free, but facts are sacred," said C.P. Scott, the famous editor of the *Manchester Guardian* from 1872 to 1929. Most news media repeat this whenever they can. It implies a clear distinction between fact and opinion, between news stories and editorial pages.

Opinion is a long-established element of the news media. Citizens rely on journalists, columnists and editors to put forward summaries, ideas and opinions. Implicit in mainstream journalism is the belief that opinion, as well as gossip and propaganda, can be kept separate from the arrangement of reports and facts in a news story.

Truth, according to mainstream journalism, can be located after all the facts have been uncovered. Some people tell lies, some exaggerate certain facts, some spout opinions with no factual basis. The duty of the journalist is to untangle all this and present the truth.

Mainstream Western journalists believe that they are paid to uphold these ideas – to be neutral, objective and factual. In return for a salary and security they will serve as a watchdog in society's best interests. The conventional wisdom among many journalists is that these concepts can be defined quite clearly and that they form the basis of good journalism. Others argue that these concepts are not so straightforward and that some of them, especially truth and unbiased opinion, don't even exist. Rather they are a convenient fiction that the news media use to maintain their power.

I would argue that objectivity, neutrality and an attempt to discern facts are an essential goal of journalism. Perhaps true objectivity and unmistakable truths remain impossible to attain. But to throw up our hands and say that everything is opinion and bias leaves us adrift and without a role in defining the media we want.

It's obvious that while the contemporary news media chant their mantra of neutrality and truth, their practice often contradicts it. Biases, ignorance and hidden agendas continually taint journalism. This holds for both owners and journalists. When journalists claim that they always report without bias, we should be skeptical. And when a news outlet says that its owner or its economic arrangements have no influence on their journalism, we can laugh.

Fortunately, the history of news journalism includes thousands of reporters, editors and even some owners who have valued fairness and truth-seeking as essential goals. They have not been satisfied by lazy reporting or official cover-ups. They have tried to act in society's best interests, not simply in the interests of commercial gain or political power. Most journalists are not heroes or, like Mercury, messengers from the gods. But a goodly number provide us with an essential service for our health and for democracy.

Chapter 2
Anatomy of the News

> It's amazing that the amount of news that happens
> in the world every day always just exactly fits the
> newspaper!
> — Jerry Seinfeld (1980s comedy routine)

We often assume that the news is what reporters and
presenters and editors tell us about current events on
TV, in the papers, on the radio and through the Internet.
Traditionally, the subject categories have been politics,
wars, economics, crime, the law and the lives of the rich
and powerful. Now we're just as apt to see stories about
ordinary people, a full range of arts and entertainment,
social trends and the always present "lifestyle" sections.
Yet, if we stop to think more about it, a precise definition
of the news becomes hard to pin down. Four standard
ingredients seem to be agreed on by journalists and editors around the world: the present tense, big consequences, sudden change and the story. I'll raise some questions
about the assumptions behind each of these elements.

The Present Tense

The news deals with the latest events. Often these events are still unfolding and the outcome is uncertain. In fact, for many news editors the best stories are those with ongoing drama. They particularly like stories with a hook at the end to keep you tuned in or online. Those stories seem to be newsworthy because they take place in a never-ending present.

Google News, for example, proudly notes beside each headline that the event being described, often thousands of miles from the newsreader, took place only so many minutes ago. This speed reflects the newest technologies as well as the large number of people involved in distributing information. Readers can receive reports directly from international news agencies, such as Reuters and the Inter Press Service, and do not have to wait for the rewrites and repackaging by the newspapers or TV stations. It's like buying goods from the factory rather than waiting for them to arrive at your local store. Media followers now expect that news will be broadcast or flow online twenty-four hours a day — there will be practically no delay in delivery to readers, listeners and viewers. In some senses the concept of news as current events is flexible. However, today's brutal push to highlight only the breaking story leads to rushed judgments (fostered by the instant analysis of news commentators) and a sense that nothing we do can stop the frenzied pace.

Big Consequences

The news concentrates on events that affect large numbers of people. Viewers, listeners and readers usually expect news items that affect the most people to lead the newscast or top the front page. That's certainly the impression that editors and producers like to convey. Major events get top billing and big type; lesser events find their place in smaller items.

Yet for all their boasts about covering the world, many huge media outlets betray an inward-looking attitude that fails to take up international issues. The US television networks exhibit this mentality most clearly. Study after study shows that people who rely on US television for news know little about the outside world, even when stories deal with issues directly affecting them.[1]

Sudden and Dramatic Change

The news gravitates toward unusual events, events out of the ordinary, events that cause a dramatic change. An old cliché of the news business expresses this: "If a dog bites a man, that's not news. But if a man bites a dog, that's news!" And these events only attract interest if the change qualifies as remarkable.

But of course there are many definitions of what's sudden and dramatic or remarkable: "Tibetan activists stage protest at Great Wall of China," "Darfur rebels agree to peace talks," "Humble snack seller is exposed as millionaire property mogul," "Spice Girl gives birth."

The news media's primary interest in sudden and dramatic change has its merits. That's because the world is an unpredictable place, full of turmoil and violence – a place where people's lives can be upended in an instant by economics, politics, and human or natural disasters. We expect the media to report these events quickly and to convey their urgency to those not involved. But what about the slow and the undramatic?

Many phenomena unfold over long stretches of time in situations that often go unnoticed. Worsening or improving health conditions are a good example. In many areas of the world cancer rates soar much higher than average and the statistics indicate growing problems. That's a story that could affect hundreds of millions. But it's not a story that the news media are normally inclined to cover. For example, in March 2007, Ghana celebrated the fiftieth anniversary of its independence from Britain. Most North American news outlets ignored it, because it didn't fit the standard news item from Africa. In Canada, the next time a powerful columnist such as the *Globe and Mail*'s Margaret Wente complains of the "corruption of Africa" and the "pointlessness" of aid and trade with the continent, who will have heard of Ghana's story and be able to register a rebuttal?

The Story

If you listen to reporters talk about their work, they always speak of the *story* they are working on, the developing *story*, the big *story*. The news creates stories about events, stories that involve people and that arrange information into a chain of cause and effect, or narrative order. The elements of urgency (or unfolding events) and consequences, along with sudden and dramatic change, only take shape when made into a story. Even business news about the stock market gets framed as part of an ongoing rise and fall that affects many people. In other words, if events can't be shaped into a story, there's a good chance they won't become news at all.

On the other hand, if a news writer or editor wants desperately enough to make something news they can usually do it by creating a story. This means putting the material together to emphasize particular elements, such as conflict, and developing a story line that creates drama, crisis, resolution and clear consequences for people.

We often think of the news as a two-step process: first, as a constant stream of events taking place "out there" in the world, and second, as the news media's knowledge-able selection of important events. But if we think of the news as stories we realize that news items aren't simply selected, they are created and constructed.

The Newsworthy

> People tend to think that journalists are where the news is. This is not so. The news is where journalists are.
>
> BBC journalist Martin Bell[2]

Drawing up a list of what the news is can take us only so far. Therefore journalists often use the term "newsworthiness." Many events *seem* to qualify as newsworthy because they include one or more of the four news characteristics of urgency, big consequences, change and story. But for some reason they never get selected. Many events involving millions of people take place around the world daily, but they don't make it to the category of news.

Why don't some stories make the news? Is there an obvious pattern of news values? Tony Harcup, a journalism professor at the University of Leeds, England, identifies several categories of stories that appear in the dominant media: the power elite, celebrity, entertainment, surprise, bad news, good news, magnitude (stories that affect many people and have a big impact), relevance (stories that editors and audiences believe matter), follow-ups (new or additional information about a previous story), media agenda (stories of particular interest to a news organization).[3]

These categories differ from the ones cited in standard journalism textbooks and by most journalists in the dominant media. In fact, many newspeople find some of Harcup's categories embarrassing. After all, categories such as celebrity and media agenda don't show the news business in the best light. Most journalism textbooks include what they call "proximity" (similar to Harcup's category of relevance) as something they consider to be newsworthy. By this they mean, how does the story relate to its audience? Is there a national angle to an international story or a local angle to a national one? Proximity implies that people become most interested in events and situations that directly affect them. To some degree this reflects an understandable human emotion. On the other hand, it projects a rather cynical view of human nature. Even those current stories that affect millions of people and that have exploded in a sudden and dramatic fashion can be swept aside when journalists overemphasize proximity as a news category.

For example, in May 2007, the US media spent forty-eight hours covering a bridge collapse in Minnesota that killed five people. Other news groups around the world picked up the story as well – it was tragic and dramatic, with plenty of startling pictures. However, at the same time floods in Bangladesh, India and Nepal, described as the worst in living memory, forced twenty million people to leave their homes. Hundreds of Asian reporters rushed to the scene, producing numerous reports and miles of good video footage. The lack of attention to the Asian story in the US thus had nothing to do with access to a remote area or long-distance technical difficulties. It simply failed to rank on the proximity scale.

Bad News Works Best

The media often seem much more interested in bad news than in good news. Most TV news centers on conflict, drama and violence, and the overall view appears to be that good news just doesn't make for compelling TV.[4]

Davis Merrit, a veteran American journalist and editor, believes that bad news dominates because it involves less risk in newsrooms.[5] Bad news stories, such as a politician taking a bribe, can be clearly verified and stay true from then on, says Merrit. On the other hand, a good news story, for instance, one that reports on the success of a particular civic program, always runs the risk of turning sour — when someone discovers that the politician behind the program wasn't quite as honest or as forthright as he or she first appeared. For that reason it's always safer for journalists to zero in on the bad. Traditionally, journalists talk about good news stories in patronizing and pejorative language — as "happy" news or "soft" news. And no one wants to appear naïve or as if they are being taken in.

The Slow News Day

There is no news tonight.
BBC radio announcer, Good Friday, 1930[6]

Sometimes you turn on the TV news and the broadcast begins with an earthquake in Pakistan that has just killed thousands. The next night the news anchor leads off by informing us that the local hospital now hands out gift baskets to all the parents of newborns. You have just experienced what's known as a "slow news day." In this case the news director has decided that nothing of significance has been happening, so the baby story will have to serve as the lead item. What this illustrates is that newsworthiness is not a fixed category that applies at all times — it depends on the competition.

In many cases, of course, big events push forward simultaneously — a war and an earthquake, for example. News editors and producers must decide which they will rank as the top priority (or at least which will be of most interest to their audience). This ordering of priorities becomes a key task for all editors and producers. A big event one day could be shunted to page seven on another, depending on what else is happening.

On a slow day minor news has a chance of making the lead item. But on a busy day the opposite takes place. On September 12, 2001, a British government communications advisor (aka spin doctor) made a big mistake. Jo Moore wrote a memo to her colleagues in government, which immediately leaked out to the press. It said, "This would be a very good day to bury bad news."[7] Predictably, the Tony Blair government showed her the door, not for what she said, but because her memo was made public.

"The news is what I say it is." This line, often attributed to US TV anchor David Brinkley, gets repeated as a matter of pride by news editors — but not usually in public. That would undercut the credo of objectivity and neutrality that is supposed to be the hallmark of the dominant media. News outlets spend considerable time trying to convince us that the news is something universal and agreed-upon from time immemorial. News, they say, takes place out there in the world and the media simply report it. Their communication to us seems straightforward. What this masks is the ongoing and active process of selection. The next time you look at a news item on TV, via the Internet, in a paper, or hear an item on the radio ask: Who decided this was news? Who made a certain event worthy, and who chose to characterize another event as unworthy?

Responsive News-Gathering

Citizens of democracies hope that their news media will be responsive to events, developments and trends, then get out to report on them. But where do journalists find their information? There are three main sources of news that journalists respond to.

Unplanned and unscripted events include accidents, disasters, wars, chance meetings, good news or bad news. For example, "Solomon Island quake triggers tsunami, at least 15 dead" (*Taipei Times*). In these situations a reporter just happens to be on the scene for an event considered newsworthy. Or an assignment editor gets a phone tip and sends a reporter scurrying to cover an event still in progress.

Planned but unscripted events include meetings to discuss or debate an issue, political demonstrations, legal trials — where the outcome is unknown, but something newsworthy could result. If producers know that a major government report or judge's decision will be released, a reporter is assigned to read it quickly and pick out the highlights. The story becomes what journalist David

Randall refers to as a "say story," that is, "A report issued this morning says that …"[8]

Planned and scripted (publicity) events include photo opportunities, press conferences, publicity tours and stunts, government and military briefings, and public speeches.[9] Historian Daniel Boorstin coined the term "pseudo-events" to describe these occasions.[10] For example, a company decides to make a donation to a local hospital (which generally means big tax benefits). The company doesn't simply send a check. It arranges a public event, signs up a TV news personality to act as master of ceremonies and hires musicians to warm up the crowd. It choreographs a ceremony with the CEO presenting a check. Everything is arranged for the TV cameras. The ceremony — known among charities as the "shake and take" — is scheduled for the late morning to give reporters enough time to munch some hors d'oeuvres and zip back to the station to package the story for the evening news. The event becomes news, and the company gets terrific publicity. In addition, the station gets to promote its newsperson MC as a caring member of the community.

Active News-Gathering

We expect that our news media will dig deeply into serious issues, ask tough questions and not be satisfied with vague or misleading answers. In contrast to passive news practices, seasoned reporters actively go out and get the news. They develop a list of contacts and informants, especially when they cover a specific subject area or beat (e.g., the city hall beat, the crime beat, the immigration beat). Contacts are called on for ideas, to provide background, and to pass on tips and gossip. Often these contacts inform the reporter on their own. In fact, good in-depth reporting can only occur through a beat reporter's reliable contacts.

Active reporting usually takes three typical forms: a straight news and information story; a feature story, involving research and background; and an investigative, purposeful story that might take years and involve real dangers. In all these forms of reporting we expect that journalists will not rely on hearsay but will search out several sources of information, that they will make every effort to be accurate, and that they will analyze the situation thoroughly enough to discover the deeper issues — not simply the surface noise. To illustrate these different forms, take the case of a major new construction project.

A straight news and information story: City government announces that a new highway will be built. A reporter follows up by interviewing all the key people in favor as well as opposed, showing exactly where the road will run, the timetable for construction, etc.

A feature story, involving research and background: The new highway becomes the subject of an in-depth article looking into its financing and the planning and history of older highway construction. We might also get more details on the companies involved in the construction. The editor assigns a photojournalist to document the progress as the highway takes shape.

An investigative, purposeful story: The new highway becomes the topic for an investigation into who stands to gain financially from the project, what homes and businesses will be affected, and how the contract was awarded to the construction company. A reporter learns that the mayor's nephew works for the construction company or that the new road will disrupt an ancient aboriginal cemetery. This news story might affect the outcome or even stop the project. We'll look at these forms of investigative reporting in more detail in Chapter 7.

Overlooked, Ignored, Suppressed

Ignoring a story can be just as significant as selecting one. It can happen through ignorance, lack of interest or as a conscious decision so as not to offend powerful business or cultural interests. Stories are overlooked or suppressed in Europe, North America, China, India — everywhere. This is because most media owners operate in close proximity to those with state power, or because reporters and editors have not found the time or interest, or because the stories don't fit the standard definitions of news.

Many types of stories miss out as news and are systematically ignored by the world's media. Industrial accidents are an example. In Canada, a worker gets killed or injured on the job every single day. These thousands of accidents rarely explode into big dramatic incidents. Rather, they take place in ones and twos, often in obscure workplaces.[11] Similarly, the mortality rates of the world's poorest children are also unreported. Most children die not from war or complicated diseases but from completely preventable illnesses such as diarrhea, caused by unclean water and poor sanitation.[12] But these stories are rarely focused on. Violence against women and white-collar crime (e.g., theft or fraud by office and professional workers), though common and widespread, also often occur as single acts in private so do not become news stories. Or they may be consciously suppressed so as not to draw attention to people in power in a society.

Reporters and editors around the world seem to agree on the basic elements of the news, but that doesn't mean that everyone handles news in the same way. Differences in the way media outlets treat the news stem from a number of factors: the characteristics of the audience, such as people's literacy levels, education, cultural differences and relative wealth or poverty; the social background and attitudes of reporters and editors, including their education and their attitudes toward news-gathering and opinion; the ownership of the news organization — state-owned, private or public corporation, or family-owned; and the national context, including government attitudes toward commercial media or the role of the government in regulating the media.

Satire and the News

The boundaries between responsible and irresponsible reporting seldom stand out clearly. And the communication of "straight" news doesn't always take the form

Chalkboard Journalism

Alfred J. Sirleaf, based in Monrovia, Liberia, writes the daily news "on a chalk board for everyone to read as they pass by on the busy main street," says newspaper analyst Juan Antonio Giner.[13] Sirleaf calls it Daily Talk and says he created it because of the need for reporting that was free and accessible to all. His newsboard was destroyed twice during Liberia's civil war (1999-2003), but now thousands of people in the capital stop to read it every day. "I do all the dirty work for them, and I give them exactly what they want," says Sirleaf.

that we're used to. Indeed, history shows that irreverent scandal sheets dedicated to satire have often played a valuable role in delivering news and "speaking truth to power" (i.e., telling people in power the facts even when they're not what they want to hear).

Irish writers Jonathan Swift, in the eighteenth century, and Oscar Wilde, in the nineteenth, showed the way. The tradition of delivering news and satire together includes widely diverse publications, such as *Punch* and *Private Eye* in Britain, *Le Canard enchaîné* in France, the *Clinic* in Chile (combining strong left-wing critiques and a *Mad* magazine style), and *Le Messager Popoli* in Douala, Cameroon.

In many countries, especially those saddled with authoritarian rule, gentle satire often provides the only outlet for social commentary.[14] In Gabon, Africa, *Le Gri-Gri International* and *La Griffe (The Claw)* have been challenging the authoritarian government for many years. They mix satirical cartoons with news stories that the government claims border on "provocation against the head of state." The editors, now exiled to France, have survived censorship, kidnap and murder attempts.

Jon Stewart's *The Daily Show* specializes in a particular form of news satire that mimics mainstream media. Stewart occupies a unique spot on American TV because he doesn't shrink from challenging powerful people and groups. Although he doesn't investigate much, he throws out a constant barrage of embarrassing questions and develops a critique of American life by probing its contradictions. Amazingly, many people hear about important news through Stewart, not via the regular news outlets.

Stretching back to early history, this alternative concept of news considers unofficial news as the only reliable news. Governments, armies and religious organizations ladle out propaganda and doublespeak. Real news, therefore, can only be trusted when it's unofficial, and low-tech. To some extent the appeal of the Internet, with its blogs and citizen journalists, flows within this tradition. The search for alternative sources reflects a worldwide discontent with the dominant media, the subject of the next chapter.

Chapter 3
The Dominant Media

At the moment we are not only generating the highest profits with our newspapers in the history of our company, but also we are making money a lot faster…

— Mathias Döepfner, Chairman of
Axel Springer AG, Germany, 2007[1]

We might assume that the statement by Mr Döepfner no longer holds. It's true that in 2009 Springer (the largest newspaper group in Europe) experienced a small decline in profits. Nevertheless, during this period it was bidding aggressively to take over Britain's *Independent*, a deal involving a billion pounds. Springer's profits in 2008 hit the highest in its 62-year history, so perhaps a small decline isn't surprising.

The news usually gets communicated to us through the filters and frames of very big companies and state-run institutions. Some groups, such as TV producers and newspaper editors and their owners, hold in their hands the power to decide what's news and what's not.

Large and powerful media institutions have been with us for more than one hundred years. At the close of the nineteenth century in Britain, newspapers such as the *Times* and the *Daily Mirror* (owned by the same family), exerted tremendous influence on both the ruling elites and the working class. Later, by the mid-twentieth century, the introduction of radio and television around the world consolidated power in very few hands, either in its state or commercial forms. The basic costs of running a major newspaper chain, TV station or radio service have restricted freedom of expression as well as the freedom to receive information from different sources to a paltry few.

Since the 1980s, however, media ownership has become lodged within an even smaller group of giants, most of which see profits as their major goal. Big now means big on a world stage, with control of both production and distribution of the news. In countries with political democracy embedded in a capitalist economy, such as most of the West and Japan, the past ten years have seen rapid changes in media ownership. That trend has been duplicated in many authoritarian countries as well, including Russia, Syria and Iran. Companies everywhere have been madly merging and buying each other out, and as a result, we now face an unprecedented concentration of ownership. Five or six giants dominate the news media in many areas of the world. Fewer and fewer companies are producing the news. It's a bad trend and poses a grave danger to democracy.

Not only do fewer owners lead to a more restricted range of views, but the vast scale of these companies makes it nearly impossible for others to jump into the game. In most cases now the scale and importance of big media require "partnerships" of the state and corporations to handle the capital required and manage the news agendas. Al-Jazeera, the leading Arab/Islamic satellite network, spent $1 billion[2] to start up Al-Jazeera English in November 2006; Sam Zell, who took control of the Tribune company, including the *Los Angeles Times*, in January 2008, had to plunk down $8.2 billion. Even that proved inadequate. Because Zell's purchase involved mostly borrowed money he went bankrupt a year later, caught up in the US bank crisis.

Another pressing danger from concentration of ownership is that journalists have limited job opportunities. When you can't easily jump ship and work elsewhere it makes you less adventurous in your reporting, threatening independence and the quality of journalism. In the US this has also greatly limited job prospects for people of color and women — both of whom are usually last-hired and first-fired — and has cut the diversity of news reporting.

Controlling access to the news allows journalists and media owners to exert influence in society — to throw their weight around. The news thus acts as bait — we read the paper or surf the net to get the news but, as in a bad recycling bin, mixed in with solid facts come opinion and spin. This control over access to information generates an important type of power that is both symbolic and quite real. That's why some media owners hold on to their newspapers even when they lose money. They know that these are businesses like no other.

News operations lend prestige to media conglomerates ordinarily focused solely on the mega-profits that flow from entertainment. In fact, this is precisely why the US TV networks launched their news divisions in the 1950s. News programs also provide legitimacy to governments that sponsor media groups. This works for Qatar's sponsorship of Al-Jazeera just as it has for decades with Britain and the BBC, Canada and the CBC, Mexico and Televisa, and Cuba and Radio Habana.

Prestige needn't curtail profits, however. Control of news distribution often leads directly to economic power and commercial gain. Most media outlets scoop up profits — until recently achieving profit margins of 20 percent to 40 percent — much higher than other businesses. Consequently, TV station ownership is often described as "a license to print money." And the $200 million annual profits of the *Los Angeles Times* before 2008 may well indicate that better management and a partial return of advertising will quickly lead back to super profits.[3] Even in the latest recession, statistics show that the US newspaper business as a whole still achieves profits of 10 percent. In many places the owners of media are some of the richest people in society. Michael Bloomberg, the billionaire head of Bloomberg financial news group and the three-time mayor of New York serves as a good example.

For this reason it makes sense to talk not simply about the *big media* but the *dominant media*. These organizations dominate the entire field of journalism and news-making. Concepts such as *mass* media or *mainstream* media give some sense of their size. But they don't convey the power of big media — the power to push other news sources to the margins or eliminate them altogether, the power to set news agendas and censor others. Referring to them as dominant reminds us how they function and reflects their position in the real world. From the US perspective, dominant equals big commercial enterprises. Elsewhere, such as in Italy, France, Mexico and India, a corporate/ state mix constitutes the dominant media. When we adopt the simplified US perspective we overlook the political influence and the power to shape or propose ideas of smaller and state-sponsored news media.

Profits and Influence

News media outlets operate as businesses, but also as opinion-shapers. Even those owned by governments, such as in China, or heavily subsidized, such as in Europe, need to function as profitably or efficiently as possible. And even those largely interested in profits wield a profound influence on the societies in which they operate.

The big media can be ranked in terms of the numbers of readers or viewers or listeners that they attract. Or they can be ranked by influence. For example, Japanese newspapers enjoy enormous circulations but their influence is primarily limited to readers in Japan. On the other hand, papers such as the *Times of India*, published in English, exert a wide international influence.

Another comparison involves commercial influence versus political influence. The world's largest newspaper chain, Metro International, of Sweden, publishes its free *Metro* papers in more than one hundred cities. Although these show little consistency in terms of content, their style and their business model have been extremely influential everywhere they have appeared. On the other hand, the papers put out by Rupert Murdoch's News Corporation wield a consistently right-wing political line. Murdoch's successful bid to take over the *Wall Street Journal* in 2007 indicates that newspaper ownership is about pushing a worldview and influence as well as about profits.

Similarly, the *New York Times*, *Le Monde* (Paris) and the *Times* (London) have much lower circulations than their more popular competitors, but their regular readers travel in the elite circles of government and business. And although the *Wall Street Journal*'s readership is comparatively

Media Giants

Three media giants have the widest general impact worldwide and generate the biggest profits. They also produce and distribute entertainment as well as news. All three are based in the US: Time Warner (includes CNN); NBC Universal, controlled by the General Electric Company; and News Corporation, controlled by Rupert Murdoch and family.

Important regional broadcasters include Central China Television (CCTV), China's state-owned broadcaster; Doordarshan, India's state-owned broadcaster; Televisa, largest producer of Spanish-language news and entertainment in Mexico, Central and South America and into the US; and DStv, a South Africa-based satellite service (not a producer) available throughout Africa.

Global broadcasters operating via satellite now reach millions of people speaking the same language. In addition to English-language broadcasters these include Phoenix Television (Hong Kong), broadcasting in Mandarin; Al-Jazeera (Qatar), in Arabic and English; Zee-TV (India), in Hindi and Urdu; TV5 (Canada) and Radio France Internationale, in French; and Globo of Brazil, the largest producer of Portuguese-language news and entertainment worldwide.

small, its subscribers earn an average of $191,000 a year.

Another group of media have kept their business focus on news and their corporate structure private or family-controlled. This allows them to claim professionalism and independence (the *New York Times*), and in some cases, a philosophy of left-liberal crusading (the *Guardian* of London and *La Jornada* of Mexico). Although their fraternity is slowly losing members to larger corporate raiders, these independent media still

Poor people listen to the radio. That's because radio is the cheapest and most reliable form of news, and also because it serves people who can't read. In Indonesia, for example, 70 percent of the population have radio. Radio in Azerbaijan reaches 99 percent of the population, in Egypt 85 percent, and in Nigeria 77 percent. Even in the least-developed countries radio use far out-ranks any other news source (by ten to one); in Mozambique radio reaches 53 percent of the population, in Rwanda 46 percent.[5]

Radio thus remains the most influential news media for the vast majority across the globe. Much of this is local or national. However, international radio news networks serve primarily as vehicles for US and European governments. Here the dominant media remain in state rather than corporate hands. Their influence has declined sharply in China, India and the Arab world, yet these networks still wield considerable influence in Africa, Eastern Europe, the Americas and parts of Asia.[6] The major radio networks are

- BBC (160 million listeners – 33 languages), 26,000 staff in Britain alone
- Voice of America (115 million listeners – 45 languages)
- Deutsche Welle, Germany (65 million listeners – 29 languages)
- Radio France Internationale (45 million listeners – 19 languages)

exert influence. But family ownership and independence from government rarely translates into a fundamental challenge to ruling elites.

Convergence

In 1999 the media world was held spellbound by a new buzz-word—convergence. The concept seemed simple. If a TV company joined with a newspaper they could cut costs, including salaries, and the result would be more power and profits. The same would apply to all sectors of the media — their convergence would open a new frontier for growth.

To name some of the biggest examples: Disney bought ABC News, General Electric bought NBC News, Rupert Murdoch set up Fox TV and took over the *Times* (London), plus the *Wall Street Journal*. Globo of Brazil and Televisa of Mexico invested heavily in new communication satellites, and in France, the arms and media conglomerate Lagardère moved in as a powerful shareholder at *Le Monde.* The idea behind these corporate moves is that economic and political dominance requires a media company to operate in many sectors of the global economy. They should not only produce content but control its distribution around the world.

One reason this has been possible is due to the convergence taking place on the technological front. In the digital age, media content using words, pictures and audio can be converted into another form. So, for example, a newspaper article can be reproduced, matched with TV images and posted online. Similarly, radio reports can become podcasts (audio broadcasts of words or music that have been converted to an audio file so they can be played back on a computer or audio player). Most big media companies now expect their reporters to work in many different media forms. In addition, the changes in technology because of the computer make long-distance distribution much easier.

Global Commerce

Over the last twenty years people have been talking about globalization — a phenomenon in which the world's economic and political systems have become more and more connected. Some analysts argue that these global systems now supersede the nation state. Corporations travel the world in search of cheaper labor and untapped markets, or new groups of people to buy their products. Actually, globalization is hardly new, but in our time it has intensified, reached further and sped up. Because most news media have in the past been nationally focused, globalization invariably creates a new situation. It opens up fresh possibilities but closes down others. Whatever the case, global trends are shaking up the old news media.

Globalization means many things but one aspect has been paramount: commercialization and a race for profits wherever they can be found. In Africa, in particular, globalization has forced governments to cut social programs, including media services, to be replaced by commercial enterprises. Global advertising has swept into Africa. Media scholar Lyombe Eko points out that most African advertising is produced in Europe by multinationals selling everything from cigarettes (using the Marlboro Man) to Mercedes Benz trucks. In fact, says Eko, "Africa is one of the last places on earth where tobacco is still advertised on radio, television, and billboards."[7]

In the US, and to some extent in Britain, Canada and France, increased global competition for profits has been accomplished in the easiest way possible: by cutting journalists from the payroll. This has been most pronounced when media investors salivate over short-term profits rather than news — casino capitalism, as they call it in Britain.

International News Flows

Big media play an influential and dominant role not only in their home countries but around the world. Many observers have characterized the results of this as a flow of news from the North to the South — from the richest countries to the poorest. It doesn't take much investigating to see that poor people in the South know much more about Europe and the US than vice versa. Usually people in the poor countries are swamped by US media, from TV to music, to celebrity shenanigans and the news. Comparatively little flows the other way, and very little flows from one place to another in the South. These patterns have existed for two or three centuries, a legacy of colonialism and a reflection of world power in general.

Some critics of the process have called these news flows a form of cultural imperialism. Internet exchange, business, science, medical and political news are all dominated by the wealthiest companies and governments. People who use the concept of cultural imperialism argue that power in the world can be enforced, not only through military and economic means, but also through the control and interpretation of information.

Yet the theories of media imperialism have been criticized on both factual and theoretical grounds. Some scholars feel that these theories divide the world into center and periphery, with the South as a bloc comprised solely of victims or dupes. Critics of the theory of cultural imperialism emphasize that within each country the upper classes and castes live a very different life than the poor. They argue that we should also consider the reality of "counter-flows" of information and news. So that rather than one dominant cultural force, situated as in the past in Western Europe or the US, several regional centers now struggle for media power.[8] Each region seems to have developed its own powerful news media that exports from one country to many others. Mexico's Televisa, Brazil's Globo, Qatar's Al-Jazeera and Hong Kong's Phoenix all play that role.

Global and Local

Sometimes global media companies operate in a crude manner. They simply pump out their homegrown news stories to other areas of the world. It's a form of dumping, where the news being offered has no value to its audience. So viewers in South America get flooded with CNN's coverage of a Kansas City murder or wildfires in California. To some extent, this is the old model of globalization.

Today, the world's dominant news providers form alliances with local or regional news outlets. Sometimes that simply involves translation of the original program into a local language. They also hire local journalists to present stories more appropriate to their audience. CNN

International uses this approach. This doesn't mean that the basic views of the company's head office get altered — it often means simply adding local color.

In a third case, American content doesn't get dumped or localized; it gets abandoned entirely in favor of local or regional programs. Even in this situation the economic relations between the US head office and local subsidiary remain in place. But many small-scale, regional and even national trends run counter to the dominant news media. The big media may be dominant but they are not omnipotent.

Chapter 4
Print, Radio and Television

My enemies have the press, so I keep television.
— French president Charles de Gaulle, 1960s

The modern news media do not dominate the news landscape solely through the economic power of their distribution and control of the market. They exploit complex aesthetic elements as well as commercial ones. In fact, all forms of the news incorporate a sophisticated understanding of communication, psychology and contemporary art, speaking to us through an impressive array of argument, persuasion and emotional involvement.

Media don't simply pass on information like the post office delivers letters. They not only deliver information, they also transform it by shaping events into genres or types of stories. Every news story can get told in many different ways — and achieves a different effect depending on whether it is told in a newspaper, on radio or on television.

The Press

The newspaper still rules as the most reliable source of news, with the most extensive coverage, for people around the world. Every day more than 515 million people worldwide buy a newspaper, and 1.4 billion people read one.[1]

Newspaper purchases have declined in North America and parts of Western Europe — in the US there was a drop of 5 percent from 2002 to 2007, to 52 million daily copies, and in Germany a drop of 2 percent, to 21 million copies. But in all other parts of the world, newspaper readership, circulation and advertising revenue show a steady rise. Japan, China and India lead the way. In India, for example, newspaper sales increased 13 percent in 2006 and over 50 percent in the previous five years.[2]

Not only are newspaper sales rising but they have made gains in global advertising revenues as well. Even in the US, where papers are suffering in the economic crisis, newspaper advertising has grown into a $40-billion business. That's twice as big as it was twenty years ago.[3] So the newspaper industry worldwide seems pretty healthy, despite the doom and gloom in some quarters.

Newspapers still devote far more time to original news-gathering than any other media. That's one reason why the current problems, such as the job cuts of journalists, attract so much attention. Newspaper coverage is broader and deeper and newspapers still employ a far greater proportion of full-time journalists than other news media. Consequently, TV and radio broadcasting,

Trouble in the US Profit Paradise

Out of business	*Rocky Mountain News* (Denver)
From print to Internet only	*Christian Science Monitor, Seattle Post-Intelligencer*
Bankrupt parents	*Chicago Tribune, Chicago Sun Times, Los Angeles Tribune*
Bailed out	*New York Times*
Bleeding badly	*San Francisco Chronicle* (losing $1 million a week in 2009)
Advertising down	18% for the industry
Job losses	Thousands of journalists, editors, assistants

as well as the Internet, remain dependent on stories generated by newspapers.

Types of Newspapers

> If a newspaper prints a sex crime, it's smut, but when the *New York Times* prints it, it's a sociological study.
> — Adolph S. Ochs, publisher of the *New York Times*

Most news vendors in major cities of the world sell what are known as broadsheets and tabloids. Throughout the twentieth century the "quality" papers were called broadsheets because of their width and their length, which require a fold. The news term "above the fold" refers to important stories on the top half of the page. The first priority for these papers was, and remains, the coverage of politics, economics and world issues. They still appeal to avid readers among the ruling elites and middle class, and continue to exert significant political influence.

The lowly tabloid — a word derived from the brand-name "condensed tablet," a nineteenth-century term for mass-produced pills — scorned by elites and intellectuals, is half the size of a broadsheet, with no fold. Tabloids provide condensed news. Right from the start, these papers rolled out a simplified and cruder journalism, often focused on scandal and sensationalism. In general their readers are less well-educated, poorer and less influential. Tabloids also incorporate much louder and more garish advertising. In fact, British tabloids are called red-tops because of their prominent red advertising bar across the top.

News stories differ to some extent in the two types of papers. Most tabloid stories are short, with clipped sentences and plain language. Often they consist of only a dozen paragraphs, all composed of one or two sentences. The stories usually fit on one page, which eliminates the need to flip ahead, and their design looks increasingly like magazines, with no stories whatsoever on the front page.

There are problems, however, with making this distinction between the two types of newspapers. Over the years the tabloids have produced some fine journalism and taken principled editorial stands. Britain's *Daily Mirror*, for example, opposed the 2003 US invasion of Iraq. And in China the boldest and most popular papers use the

Famous Broadsheets	Famous Tabloids
Le Monde (France)	*Bild-Zeitung* (Germany)
The Guardian (Britain)	*The Daily Mirror* (Britain)
The New York Times (US)	*The New York Post* (US)
The Times of India (India)	*Clarín* (Argentina)
La Jornada (Mexico)	*The Advertiser* (Australia)

tabloid format. Broadsheets also print their share of sleaze and sensation, so to some degree, the difference in paper format boils down to one of style and cultural interests.

Hard News

Hard news stories can be based on either a response to events or an active approach. The items start with what's called a "lead," a sentence or paragraph that lays out, right off the bat, the five Ws — the what, where, who, when and why. From that beginning the story resembles an inverted pyramid. It spells out the most vital information at the top and provides the least important near the end. According to this model readers who want only the basic information will find it in the first two or three paragraphs. Readers who choose to continue can stick with it, as more and more specific or minor details get filled in. This model allows editors to easily cut the item for length, starting at the bottom. It also allows the quickest and most flexible means of translation to another medium, say from print to a website. A ten-paragraph newspaper item might get chopped to twenty words in a text message.

Reporters write these items in the third person and never refer to themselves. The idea is to present the story in a form that looks as objective and unbiased as possible. There is much to be said for this clear, direct style. But language always carries other meanings. In this case the implication is that the content is true and that no one appears to have selected or shaped the story.

In hard news stories descriptions of people and settings only appear if they are essential to the story. They always mention the date and place. And increasingly, because of twenty-four-hour all-news delivery, they indicate the exact time that an event took place and when the story was posted or written. In the old days reporters could use the past tense, but competition from TV, radio and the web have forced a more immediate writing style. Now you read "Car bomb kills 10 in Baghdad," "Business leaders meet to discuss …"

Reporters follow many basic routines in news-gathering and writing up these stories. Statements from newsmakers or eye-witnesses always get written up in quotation marks. ("'The mayor is just trying to line his pockets,' says a local business-owner.") This makes the story feel "true" and protects the journalist. By putting questionable or biased or outrageous statements in quotes the journalist can liven up the story and appear to be simply passing on one person's view. These quotations usually get balanced with others that take a different or conflicting view. ("In reply, the mayor stated, 'I never made a penny on those deals.'") This charge and counter-charge format allows the reporter to claim a balanced, fair or unbiased story.

Features

Feature writing gives journalists an opportunity to write longer stories and to delve into the background or context. Although features deal with current events, in most cases the time-frame is extended. Features provide readers with more of the "whys" behind a news story or explain the significance of events. In addition, features are not locked into any particular style. Sometimes they delay the lead and start instead with an anecdote, sketching in a setting or describing a person. This "soft-lead" style appears increasingly in hard-news stories as well. Features often read like short stories, making ample use of narrative devices. For instance, they might withhold information, create conflict, follow one person, build to a climax or end with a "kicker" — a surprising or shocking ending.

Many features don't simply describe; they establish a scene. This follows a general trend in writing sometimes called "creative nonfiction." In addition to using narrative and drama, creative nonfiction brings the writer into the story and includes her or his thoughts and feelings. This never happens in the hard-news approach.

Editors usually vary the types of features they run.[4] Personality profiles mix interview and observation as well as creative writing and editorializing. Human interest stories and trend stories deal with everything from popular fads to suggestions for better ways to live. In-depth stories use research and interviews and recap major news. A backgrounder or an analysis piece provides an historical overview or fills out the context of a current issue.

Headlines

One of the most valued skills in a newsroom is the ability to write headlines. A sub- or copy-editor, not the reporter, usually performs this role and provides some continuity of style throughout the paper. Headlines often suggest in a subtle way how the reader should interpret the news story below. It's a form of masked editorializing that reflects the editor's or owner's point of view and signals a paper's identity or "brand" image.

The tabloids love brash phrases: "It may shock you, but it must be told!" A headline can turn a straight news story into a joke, using puns or alliteration, like this one involving steroid use from the tabloid *Toronto Sun*: "Roid rage? Drugs found in wrestler's home after murder-suicide." A headline can personalize an issue, even when the reporter has taken pains not to. For example, a reporter may have covered a farm community meeting and noted that many people expressed opinions. But the headline simplifies and personalizes things by announcing, "Gonzalez triumphs over Ramirez in close vote." Headlines often emphasize conflict and flatten complex stories into sensational catch phrases.

Images

> It is clear enough by now to most people, that
> "the camera never lies" is a foolish saying. Yet it is
> doubtful whether most people realize how extraor-
> dinarily slippery a liar the camera is.
>
> James Agee[5]

Just as literacy and the power of the text have expanded
worldwide so has the proliferation of images, above all
through the news media. Without the power and immediacy of photographs, could the news media remain a
mass medium? I doubt it. Most of us would take much
less interest if the news did not include photography. It
is also photography that delivers the audience to advertisers. Thus, *The Canadian Press Stylebook* points out that
"A good picture can carry a story onto page one; lack of a
picture can take a good story ... right out of the paper."[6]

Machine-based images, in contrast with their hand-
drawn predecessors, carry the authority of truth. Even
when we know that images can be doctored and manipu-
lated, we still fall into the belief that the mechanical
image cannot lie. For that reason photographs go hand-
in-hand with the mythology of a professional, objective
point of view. Photography also broadens the news
agenda, bringing us into contact with everyday events
and ordinary people. It can show us the details of settings and places as well as moods, relationships and feelings. Unlike nineteenth-century newspapers, newspapers

today no longer focus exclusively on the doings of the rich and powerful.

The dominant news media also use the new forms of "amateur" photography as a means of drawing in readers and viewers. By incorporating pictures from cell phones and digital cameras, news editors and producers hope to prove that their organization is hip, interactive and in touch with youth.

Photojournalism

All newspapers and most news magazines incorporate photographs into their news practices, mostly a routine single illustration accompanying a story. Photojournalism attempts to give more weight to the photographs, using images to add an extra dimension or new meaning to a piece. In its most expansive form photojournalism involves a series of photos that tell a story or present an argument, like a visual essay.

Germany pioneered the illustrated newspaper or picture press, and in the 1920s more than a dozen vied for attention. *Life* magazine, which was published in the US from 1936 to 2000, probably did the most to popularize photojournalism by expanding on the German tradition. *Life* revealed situations or provided testimony previously unknown. From the 1960s, for example, Gordon Parks' beautifully striking visual essays of the African American experience in Harlem portray everyone from office cleaners to Malcolm X and Muhammad Ali.

Although most photographers would like to be

known as photojournalists, the news outfits they work for rarely allow much opportunity. American magazines such as *National Geographic* and *Time*, *Paris Match*, *Geo* and *Stern* in Germany, along with a few quality Sunday papers, provide the best sites for this type of visual news.[7] Yet many important photojournalists experience great difficulty in placing their work in mainstream news venues. Instead, their photos often appear in small magazines or reports of NGOs, such as the Red Cross or Doctors Without Borders. This is an important reminder that the news doesn't always travel through the dominant media.

Photographic images play an essential role in today's delivery of print and television news. But as James Agee reminds us, the camera can be a slippery liar — and photographers and editors have at their disposal a potent means of shaping the news. Although they can distort information, photographic images can also deliver a remarkably direct and powerful knowledge of the world beyond our own reality. The best news photographers bring us new knowledge and understanding that is impossible to convey through words alone.

Non–News

News makes up on average only 40 percent of newspaper content. Some papers carry much less. Just the ads alone gobble up a huge proportion of space, charging at us in three basic forms: display ads, classified ads and ads masquerading as stories. The story-form ads usually appear in the fashion, auto, technology, real estate and lifestyle sections. They're basically product promotions with photos supplied by the seller and with text only slightly rewritten from press releases. For example, a survey of world newspapers in March 2008 shows dozens with front-page stories, complete with color pictures, of the newly released Apple iPhone. The insider term for this kind of journalism, where writers churn out rewrites of press releases, is churnalism.

Chicago's Robb Montgomery was hired in 1995 to develop a new tabloid called *Red Streak*. He explained his task without mentioning news: "We were willing to take big risks but we also made sure we sailed the seven 'C's. The seven 'C's that help build habits: Columnists, Crosswords, Classified, Comics, Celebrity, Channels (TV listings), Color (like the weather page)!"[8] Montgomery's reference to building habits should remind us that modern news media need us to keep coming back – tomorrow or to the next edition or the next hour. They work hard to develop our "brand loyalty," a practice that shapes many news genres. We know their slogans by heart: stay tuned, join us tonight, sign up for our newsfeed, keep it locked.

Journalism students at San José State University in California have quantified many of these trends, including the use of superficial stories and non-news, on a website called Grade the News. In a 2006 report they conclude, "After watching more than a thousand TV stories, our overall impression was that local stations are extremely good at covering the least important news of the day – random action events such as episodes of violence, fires and accidents."[9]

Radio News

More people worldwide listen to radio news than any other medium. This is especially true of the poor. Compared to other forms it's the least expensive, especially for listeners, and it can be portable and sent over long distances or rough terrain. Reporters can gather material with little fuss and — by using a small recorder that is less visible than taking notes — under the radar of authorities.

Mainstream radio news generally runs in short programs, often five minutes or less. Each newscast consists of several items, usually about thirty seconds in length. A regular newsreader, who introduces herself or himself, provides consistency and links the items with short transitional phrases. For stations with reporters the studio reader usually sets up the story then throws it over to the staff reporter. Unlike newspaper hard-news stories, based on the inverted pyramid, radio and TV items need to be much shorter. And not only must they grab your attention right away, they must hold your interest for the entire story. For that reason many radio and TV clips end with a strong, clear phrase called a "snapper."

Some well-financed, state-funded radio operations, such as the BBC, Radio France-Internationale and the Canadian Broadcasting Corporation, offer longer news reports. These often get updated every hour and include interviews, some live, some taped. The location stories usually also mix

Farm Radio International

Farm Radio International is a non-profit Canadian group that aims to fight poverty and food scarcity.[10] It works in direct partnership with approximately 300 radio broadcasters in 39 African and Asian countries. For example, VISCA Radio in the Philippines operates a School on the Air (SOA) for farmers. "SOA requires that farmers who register apply most of the techniques that they learn during the course," says Adelina Carreno, the director. "So far the station has conducted more than twenty Schools on the Air on various farm topics. Thousands of farmer students have participated," says Carreno. The only tool needed is a radio.

in audio of background sounds to lend ambiance and mood. For instance, while a reporter describes a scene in downtown Karachi, you'll hear street sounds, other voices, perhaps car horns. These may be live or recorded earlier and edited to play under the reporter's words.

In the world's poorest areas, in countries with low literacy rates and poor access to telephone service, local radio performs an essential public service.

Talk Radio

In Uganda, following the start-up of commercial radio during the 1990s, radio stations threw themselves into cutthroat competition. This led to some novel experiments, such as the free speech phenomenon known as bar-room broadcasting.

"Radio stations saw an opportunity to increase their ratings," explains Lyombe Eko. "Many headed for the bars.... The resulting alcohol-fueled debates, which took place in a mixture of dialects and languages, were broadcast live. All topics were fair game…. When debaters started being disrespectful or insulting toward the president… a jittery Ugandan government threatened to ban live broadcasts."[11]

Most talk radio is even simpler than this and doesn't require anyone to leave the studio. That makes it cheap to produce, especially with a phone-in format. In North America an occasional interview or eyewitness account can bring to light an important event or piece of information. Sadly, however, very little news makes its way onto these shows. And because talk radio counts as "public affairs," and therefore fulfills the station's license obligation to offer some public service (news that's essential to listeners), it has pushed genuine news to the margins. The smaller stations simply grab, then compress, their stories from the local newspapers, with public service confined to traffic and weather. The morning DJ comes in early to read the papers, works up some headlines and, presto, the news is ready to go.

Not all commercial radio has sunk this low, but even in the US, where the major broadcasters used to run decent radio news, the amount of news has drastically declined. Much has been replaced by extreme right-wing opinion shows that unashamedly strut what many critics define as right-wing, sexist, racist and homophobic views. For most listeners "talk radio" means harsh, vindictive shouting and the lowest forms of public discourse, giving people such as Don Imus and Howard Stern a giant platform and enormous power. Clear Channel Communications, a private corporation and the largest radio group in the US with 900 stations, plays a leading role in promoting the agenda and biases of the far right with dozens of similar shows—Rush Limbaugh, the current top dog, pulls in 20 million listeners per day.

Public Radio

Public radio usually operates with state funding. But unlike directly controlled state organizations, such as Iran's Broadcasting Service or the US-run Voice of America, public stations enjoy a good deal more editorial independence. Many public stations draw in corporate sponsors and individual donors as well. The BBC, which was launched in the 1920s, provides the best-known model for this service and is heard around the world.

In Europe, after the Second World War, nearly all countries set up public radio and TV funded by government but with varying degrees of freedom. In the US the National Public Radio (NPR) network functions in a similar way, but with ever-increasing reliance on corporate sponsors.[12] NPR and a few small university and community stations, such as Pacifica in California and WBAI in New York, are the only places on the US airwaves where truly dissenting voices can be found. Although somewhat independent, these stations must walk a fine line in the way they treat news. They can't stray too far from the mainstream or they risk losing their government or corporate funding. And although they face increasing pressures to make more money, they must continually prove that they are not "competing unfairly" with commercial radio.

Television News

A 2007 British study showed that the number of young people who watch TV news had dropped by half since 2000. Two-thirds said the news was not relevant to them.[13] Nevertheless, in Western Europe, North America and other wealthy parts of the world such as Japan, Australia, Israel and Argentina, more people get their news from television than any other source. It comes in two flavors: the traditional regular-time broadcasts and the newer twenty-four-hour formats.

Regular Broadcasts

Most stations offer regular news programs three or four times a day — morning, noon, supper-hour and evening. Each of these slots presents the stories in slightly different ways, with different anchors or newsreaders. They do this partly for variety and partly to attract specific audiences. Traditionally, the daytime slots mix key national and international stories with considerable amounts of human interest and light fare. The supper and evening slots focus more on politics, business and international stories. Originally, this difference in focus supposedly mirrored the fact that more men watched at night.

News program producers and editors think very carefully about the lineup of stories. A number of factors

Global TV Giants

Al–Jazeera	CNN	BBC (largest broadcaster)
Founded in 1996	Founded in 1980	Founded in 1928
150 million viewers	260 million viewers	150 million TV, 160 million radio
Arabic and English	15 languages	33 languages
Qatar private corporation	US corporation	Public
Critical of US	Pro US / Israel	Pro British / Israel
Critical of Arab states	Critical of Arab states	Critical of Arab states
Dominant in Middle East	Dominant in world	Dominant in radio worldwide
1,200 journalists	4,000 journalists	2,000 journalists in UK
Limited international reporting	Some international reports	Extensive international reports/bureaus

influence the lineup. The first factor is time. For commercial stations the normal thirty-minute program includes four breaks for ads. This gives the show five segments, and each segment, except the last short one, needs four or five stories. Using this segment format, producers like to group stories that are similar in tone and place. In other words, they don't jump back and forth between tragic and light or between local and international. Similar stories also create a flow that provides smooth transitions and encourages viewers to keep watching.

In traditional newscasts the significant hard news was followed by less important items, the "We leave you

Al-Jazeera English
- Style: modeled on the BBC — authoritative, sober, relatively long segments, subtle bias of world view in the scripts ("Following the failed US policy in Iraq ...")
- Leading programs: twenty-four-hour rolling news, *Witness, 101 Asia* (short international issues reports and documentaries)
- Political orientation: independent pan-Arab, gently critical of the US and specific policies of Arab governments

CNN English
- Style: very fast-paced, short segments, opulent studio sets and special effects
- Leading programs: twenty-four-hour rolling news, featuring Lou Dobbs, Anderson Cooper, Soledad O'Brien
- Political orientation: pro-US, with a mix of commentators — from the center (Larry King) to the far right (Glenn Beck / Nancy Grace)

with this strange story" technique. Now, however, the newscast unfolds more like a variety show, supplying jolts and highlights at key points throughout. Producers often hold back something particularly newsworthy or sensational in order to create a "wow" finish.

Reporters and Readers

TV news began life as nothing much more than a radio script being read by a serious-looking man in a suit behind a desk.[14] The newsreader, presenter or anchor remains a key element in TV news. Over the years stations have experimented with every kind of news desk, camera angle and framing strategy. For some newscasts the anchor now leaves the desk and stands for key moments or even the entire program. Regardless of the set-up, the most important element is the authority of the anchor. After all, anchors represent the station, the network and journalism in general. They are the face that legitimizes the news organization in its role as Fourth Estate, equivalent to other groups in society.[15] The anchor must be likeable, telegenic, acceptable to sponsors and a magnet for high ratings.

The only other group in TV news with the visual status to approach the audience head-on is the reporters. This gives them the same type of authority as the presenters. Anyone else on camera, even important newsmakers, must look slightly off-camera or speak sideways to a reporter. Reporters rank second only to the anchor as the public face of the news organization. TV news organizations go to great lengths to build up the image of their reporters. They don't need to be as photogenic as the anchors, and sometimes a weather-beaten appearance adds street credibility, but generally reporters look good on camera, sporting stylish hair and perfect teeth. Ads and slogans for the news department promote the reporters' work and push them forward as celebrity professionals.

In China, for example, Hong Kong-based Phoenix TV actively promotes journalist newsreader Rose Luqiu as a celebrity. They sent out this press release in 2006: "Phoenix reporter Rose Luqiu must surely be a role model for all Chinese journalists. She was the first Chinese journalist to enter Baghdad in 2003 to report the war in Iraq and she was selected as one of the twenty 'Most Envious [sic] Chinese women' in France's *Madame Figaro* Magazine."

Anchors and key reporters regularly fly off on prestige field assignments (dangerous but not too dangerous) to display their journalistic skills. Donning a flak jacket and jeans and cutting back on the make-up helps show their seriousness. Everyone works hard to refute the popular notion that the anchor is just a pretty face, not a real journalist.

Back in the studio, sets have evolved from bare and drab backdrops to elaborate, over-the-top theatrical productions. Even small-scale local news programs like to show off their set and production facilities. The scale of the set seems to reflect the resources of the station and its connection to a vast electronic world of news-gathering. A back wall of TV monitors and international clocks is a favorite design, with numerous people hurrying past in the background to give the feeling of perpetual activity. The news never stops. Viewers never see people just sitting at desks and writing the scripts, and this is as true at Al-Jazeera as everywhere else. That would imply that the news is as much a created product as a series of constantly breaking outside events.

The News Screen

Not only has the studio changed, the TV screen itself has become more elaborate. In the 1980s video effects made it easier to combine images on-screen. Since the 1990s the TV news presentation resembles a computer screen. Now the presenter gets framed off-center to make room for computer graphics, maps, logos, menus and reports from off-site reporters. Again, an off-center, slightly unbalanced image conveys an impression of action — up-to-the-minute, suddenly exploding events. "Wow," we say, "these folks are really scrambling to keep us informed." Additional information or top story headlines crawl across the lower third of the screen and the station logo hovers in a prominent place for the entire broadcast. Many stories now include an on-screen descriptive tag-line between the scroll-bar and the main images. Tag-lines resemble newspaper headlines, but are shorter, often using just two or three words: "Jetliner Crash," "Warming Oceans," "New Business Tax," "Crisis in Pakistan."

The visual material is designed to impress viewers with the complexity and fast-moving nature of the news. It also reflects the sophisticated technology that only an organization like this one can handle. Visual references to the computer screen transform the "old" technology of TV into something "cool" and youthful. Ironically, of course, as all studies show, newscasts generally attract older audiences, who often experience this as so much clutter and glitz.[16]

The Rolling News

Newspapers operate on a daily news schedule. Radio tries to run fresh newscasts every hour. And until the birth of Ted Turner's CNN, in 1980, TV ran on a three or four times a day schedule. Now, however, many TV broadcasters operate rolling newscasts — all news all the time. This has altered TV news in particular and has affected all the other media as well.

The twenty-four-hour news differs from regularly scheduled programs in several key areas. The constantly rolling format puts more emphasis on the very latest stories and developments. Consequently, reporters have less time to prepare and to undertake some of the traditional news-gathering techniques, such as double-checking facts, seeking second opinions and providing background. The scramble to get the story on the air encourages the coverage of live or unfolding events, and rushing a reporter to the scene becomes the highest priority. Naturally for really big, "breaking" stories viewers turn to the twenty-four-hour newscasts. They're exciting and seem to provide us with direct, unmediated access. They haven't yet been scripted in the studio or explained by the experts or spun by the PR specialists. That's a big part of the appeal.

The other important difference from regular news broadcasts is the mix of story type and tone within each time-block. Twenty-four-hour news loves to interrupt itself and switch to a "breaking story, just coming over the wires," something that may have no connection to what's currently on-screen. Rather than holding the attention of audiences through a careful flow of related stories, the rolling news holds out the promise of constant surprise or shock.

If you watch the twenty-four-hour news closely, however, you find that the momentous, breaking story doesn't take place as often as you might think. Twenty-four-hour news incessantly repeats the same information. And it constantly throws out teasers, such as, "We're just about to go live." It also excels at parceling out tiny morsels of information one bite at a time. One piece now and another, as they say on CNN, "straight ahead, right after the break."

More than any other phenomenon, twenty-four-hour news has shaken the news business in all sectors. Regular news broadcasts and newspapers find that their standard hard-news stories feel old and tired. With the exception of active, investigative reporting that reveals newsworthy information, the twenty-four-hour folks always seem to get there first.

Local News

"The Pope is Dead but the Yankees are Still Alive: Details at 11:00"

Local news makes a great target for satire but at its best it fulfills an important role in society. After all, most of us aren't jet-setters. We live locally and local news often affects us and our neighbors personally. The joke about the Pope and the Yankees baseball team sums up the way local news looks at the world. Local news takes national or international stories and finds the local angle. Or editors dig up a local story that they hope will get picked up by a network. But their mandate centers on the content — local above all.

Local TV news has suffered in North America and Britain since the 2008 economic crisis. But the cuts to staff, programs and even stations stretches back many years. In Canada, for instance, major cuts accompanied the recessions of 1994, 2000 and 2009.

The success of a local program depends greatly on its studio talent. Local newscasters almost never present stories on their own. They're part of a team. A man and woman read the main news, accompanied by the quirky weather person, the fast-talking jock and the bubbly favorite who covers entertainment. The show features a lot of light-hearted joking and kidding. Sometimes the banter sets the scene for a little flirting, where the man and woman play the roles of a familiar, but not married, couple. This chemistry, or lack of it, quickly gets translated into ratings and affects the advertising money. Advertisers generally prefer radio and TV stations that carry some mix of information and entertainment.

Local news often tries to strike a different tone from the national news. Rather than focusing on the tragic, the scary, the bewildering and the bad, local news regularly produces "good news" stories or "Happy News." To some extent this responds to audience surveys that complain that the news is "too depressing," or "the media are just too cynical." Happy News tries to answer these critiques but often comes across as trite entertainment. Cities have serious problems with massive poverty, injustice and oppression. Happy News ignores all that.

Local news loves the slogan, "news you can use."

Of course, reporting the news in a way that makes connections between the story and the viewers' lives is effective and informative. For example, a story about a local refugee family can be expanded to explain where the family has come from and why they are fleeing. Conversely, a big world event that takes place in India can be the occasion to introduce viewers to local Indian communities.

The problem with "news you can use," as with the Happy News phenomenon, is that too often it becomes an excuse to bury one's head in the sand, sticking to the local when the community desperately needs a wider perspective. Much of this parochial news centers on lifestyle or consumer issues — how to buy a car, new fads in health care or nifty home renovations. A steady diet of these issues, to the exclusion of the more traditional hard news, means that citizens lack the information they need to participate in a true democracy. For example, in the area of public health a local news show might report unusually high cancer rates in one neighborhood, but neglect to investigate further. If they did they might find similar problems in other parts of the country and become aware of patterns, or begin to see that a known industrial polluter once operated near their area.

Morning Formats — Breakfast Television Rising
Almost every country in the world has a breakfast TV show. They all seem to follow the same format, mixing serious interviews and silliness with weather and traffic.

Breakfast TV is generally broadcast live and uses a living-room or kitchen-style set (not a news-studio or office set). It has a magazine format, jumping from one subject or tone or geography to another that is entirely different. Britain's *TV-AM* was for many years noted for its mascot, Roland Rat. There's *Breakfast Supersize* in the Philippines, *Telediario Matinal* in Spain, *Good Morning Nippon* in Japan and *Cock-a-doodle-doo* in Trinidad and Tobago, among others. These programs feature regular segments outside in the streets, showing reporters mixing with their viewers, who wave and cheer. "You see," says the station, "we are one with our audience."

Many breakfast shows pull in higher ratings and achieve more commercial success than other news or current events programs in the lineup. The *Today* show on NBC draws 6 million viewers daily and brings in $350 million a year. That's three times more than the prime-time news shows.[17]

Chapter 5
The Internet

Online news sources have multiplied substantially since 2000, and the Internet buzzes with predictions about the death of the old news media. As computer use accelerates and fast broadband connections become widely available, media companies are changing the way that the news is delivered. Not only that, citizens of all kinds have begun to write, report and distribute news of their own.

The special features of the Internet have the potential to change many characteristics of news itself, opening up fresh possibilities and creating broader expectations about journalism. In fact, the newest online forms, especially the social networking media such as Facebook, YouTube and Twitter, now work as important news conduits, especially for young people. And because these sites connect like-minded people, it seems to many of their users that the social media operate separately from the dominant news media. Users can simply move on when authorities or overly commercial operators move in.

All this poses an enormous challenge to the dominant news business. Some editors and journalists in TV, print and radio react with fear or scorn. They contend that these new "amateur" forms of news, where anyone can voice an opinion and no one steps forward to edit, will discredit all journalism. Others claim that great amounts of material that appear online can't be trusted when written and posted exclusively by one person. Only the well-established institutions, they say — such as the BBC, with its internal checks and balances — can be relied on to report on serious and complex issues and be held accountable for what they produce.

But not everyone in the dominant media views online news as a threat. Many in the business see the potential of extending the reach of the old companies to provide better news coverage and operate on a global scale. Joan Connell of MSNBC says, "Now anyone with something to say and access to the right software can be a publisher, a pundit and observer of events great and small."[1]

Yet this is surely an overstatement about democratic trends in media. Clearly, a reporter for a major news outfit carries the enormous power and clout of a dominant institution. And company connections provide a guest pass to places of power that would be closed to the average do-it-yourself online journalist.

Defenders of the dominant media argue that the Internet provides space for everyone to express their views and communicate their cultural values. At the same time many strong critics of the dominant media argue that the Internet allows us to receive and transmit information and ideas without all the middlemen and gatekeepers who populate the mainstream news business. For many of its promoters, this online newsworld is a positive symbol of globalization and the competitive capitalist system, demonstrating that almost anyone can jump into the media game. These defenders of the dominant media believe that Marshall McLuhan's 1960s prediction of a Global Village has finally come to pass.[2] Not only can we receive information from far away, but we can speak and work with others directly, no matter how distant their homes.

Special Features

Despite what we may think of the promises made by the advocates of online news, this newly emerging digital world does contain exciting characteristics that sets it apart from older news forms.[3] Online news has the potential to combine different forms of communication — text, sounds and images. In addition, online news sites allow users to speak and listen to others in real time, to carry on a real conversation. Of course, this combination of oral and text-based communications remains only potential for most online sites.

Although the term "interactive" has been shamelessly hyped, especially by those who sell computers and software, the world of online communication does provide opportunities for two-way conversations. No longer need we be passive consumers of what the experts deem newsworthy. We can talk back. We can also modify the forms by which we receive the news, for example, through customized news feeds and alerts. Finally, we have the ability to create and distribute our own news — news that might reach many, many people.

Simply by clicking on a standard source such as Google News, anyone now has access to hundreds of articles from newspapers all over the world, many we've never heard of, let alone read. A slightly more knowledgeable web surfer can draw on archives, blogs, podcasts, wikis, maps and image banks from photojournalists to gather information and opinions far beyond the dominant sources. For example, people interested in background on the turmoil in Zimbabwe can read the Guardian Unlimited's lead online story then link to more than 400 previous articles, with photos and video, about the contentious March 29, 2008, election and violence.

For people living in repressive or authoritarian countries the Internet has been hailed as a means of connecting to and communicating with the outside world. News, images, data and opinion now range freely across national borders. The problem, however, has been privacy, because police and the military are masters of eavesdropping and surveillance. Many journalists and political activists have played an ongoing game of cat and mouse with the authorities. Sometimes the police get the upper hand and shut down websites or make arrests. Other times, at least for a while, activists can evade the censors.

Repressive governments have many ways to censor or block Internet news and discussions. For example, as journalist Becky Hogge points out, "When Internet surfers in South Korea type in a url to take them to a North Korean website, they are automatically redirected to a site run by the South Korean police. As if that weren't scary enough, the site is programmed to flash the user's own IP address back."[4] The authorities are watching.

News Sources

Online news has been developed by two types of organizations: the new groups that have created stand-alone websites and the established media companies that have created specialized news sites or have developed online versions of their existing newspapers, television stations and radio networks.

Sites created by new companies or organizations include Google News, Yahoo News, Global Voices and allAfrica.com (US), OhmyNews (Korea) and Rabble (Canada) among many others. These sites range from the very biggest readership to organizations with tiny audiences. The biggest operate around the clock while the smallest publish on a magazine schedule, with new content usually added weekly. Some sites created by old-media owners provide a new type of service and include some original content. Examples include MSNBC, a world leader with 23 million monthly visitors; Thomson Reuters News Agency; *The Irish News* TV service (Belfast); and IRIN (Integrated Regional Information Networks, published by the United Nations, presenting news on Africa and Asia).

Sites of existing media organizations include the BBC, the *Boston Globe, Le Monde,* the *Australian* and thousands of others. Some create new content but many simply dump their regular stories into the site. This goes by the derogatory name of "shovel-ware." Many small radio, newspapers and television outlets operate this way.

But it is the aggregator sites — such as Google, Yahoo and AOL — that are truly innovative. Although none of them have their own journalists, they bring together and juxtapose news from a range of sources, then rank and display it, often creating startling forms of fresh knowledge. When you have the *New York Times* and the *Daily Champion* of Lagos, Nigeria, both reporting on the same story, you get a wider and deeper perspective.

Blogs

A growing number of online news sources stretch the

boundaries of news and push the differences with traditional media much further. The weblog, or blog, is a type of journal with links, combined with an invitation for readers to comment. Blogs have gained so much attention that the word has spawned new grammatical offspring, such as "blogger" and "blogosphere," the "place" where blogging takes place. In 2006 the term "blogola" entered the lexicon to describe the situation of bloggers taking money from politicians and corporations in return for favorable coverage or promotion of a product.

The concept of a journal, or diary, actually an old form, implies something casual, often conversational in tone. It allows a personal voice and often features impressions rather than verifiable facts or a tightly argued essay. Many blogs function as simple diaries with short blasts of opinion, neither of which qualify as news. The best provide a running commentary on current events and function as a remarkable resource, like a helpful librarian or hip sister — making links and connections or pointing out untapped sources of information.

There are three main types of blogs, each delivering what I'd define as news: old-pundit blogs, participant blogs and citizen journalists online. Blogs from the old-media journalists and celebrities make up one category. People such as Katie Couric, of CBS, and Anderson Cooper, of CNN, already rich and powerful, use blogs to further extend their reach. But their blogs are so clogged by commercial messages that it's hard to see why anyone searching for new information would bother. In 2007

Couric and her CBS News bosses were embarrassed when it was revealed that she didn't actually write her own blog. But the fact that she needed one shows how important blogging has become. Being an articulate, photogenic newsreader no longer provides enough credibility.

Participant blogs, where the reporter is also an active, even partisan participant, have been created by the thousands. Some of the most interesting are the warblogs created by soldiers and others. Naturally, the dominant media give plenty of airplay to US soldier heroes. A more interesting example is *Where is Raed?* by Salam Pax, the pseudonym of a twenty-nine-year-old Iraqi architect who wrote as an "embedded citizen" in Baghdad during the build-up to the 2003 US invasion.[7] He was later hired by the *Guardian* to write a newspaper column and by a British film company who turned his blog writings into a new form of video diaries. In 2003 he published his blogs in a book called *The Baghdad Blog*.[8]

A 2005 estimate claims there are 75,000 active blogs coming out of Iran (where 70 percent of the population is under thirty), mostly in Persian.[9] Iranian bloggers face the danger of censorship, arrest and torture by the authorities for blogs deemed subversive. Yet the government's inability to shut down the political blogosphere remains an embarrassment. Some leaders see it as a Trojan horse, bringing subversive ideas and Western culture into their midst. RezBiz, an Iranian, writing in *My Other Fellow,* says: "With almost all Iran's reformist newspapers closed down and many editors imprisoned, blogs offer an opportunity for dissent, discussion and dissemination of ideas that is not available in any other forum. I keep a weblog so that I can breathe in this suffocating air."[10]

Citizen Journalists Online

Online news sites have not only encouraged more people to get into the act, they have also spawned new types of journalism. In Korea, OhmyNews, and OhmyNews International, in English, were set up in 2000 by successful businessman Oh Yeon-ho. The OhmyNews motto is "Every Citizen is a Reporter." Mr Oh, a long-time critic of the government, explains: "My generation were in the streets fighting in the 1980s against the military dictatorship. Now, 20 years later, we are combat-ready with our Internet. We really want to be part of forming public opinion."[11] Some Koreans credit OhmyNews with Roh Moo-hyun's win in the 2006 presidential election. Moo-hyun was the underdog until the reporters and editors of OhmyNews gave him their support. Although Korea still has a conservative mainstream media linked to powerful business and military elites, it also has the highest percentage of people linked to the Internet, nearly 70 percent — so net journalism can play a big role.

Lily Yulianti, a "citizen reporter" in Indonesia, launched Panyingkul (Intersection) in 2007. Ms. Yulianti says that "this model channels citizens' voices and promotes people's involvement in the public arena." Panyingkul covers social issues such as street children and the urban poor as well as education, arts and literature.[12]

Wikinews, a spinoff of the fabulously successful Wikipedia, also allows anyone to write and edit the articles. As a result, all articles are the product of many writers. The editors encourage both synthesis articles and original reporting. Wikinews strives for a complete separation of news and opinion. In the language of Wiki, all articles should be NPOV (non-point-of-view). Of course, objectivity may be fine as a goal but it is rarely achieved. A complete range of viewpoints seldom takes place and thus Wikinews, like all other forms of journalism, depends to some degree on the writer.

Podcasts

A podcast is a form of Internet radio available to subscribers. When a podcaster (that's a person) creates and posts a new program it streams out to all subscribers simultaneously. That makes it different from conventional radio in two ways. First, it doesn't get transmitted via sound waves through the atmosphere and, second, it is not broadcast for anyone to pick up. You can't stumble onto a podcast in the same way you find stations by scanning the radio dial.

Unfortunately, the term podcast derives from a commercial product, the Apple iPod, and Apple has done its best to profit from the phenomenon, for example by suing other groups from using the word "pod." Still, inexpensive technology makes podcasting popular, and the practice has also gained an audience among left and liberal followers of the news, largely because so much radio, especially the US-style commercial fare, remains tightly controlled by a very few companies. Podcasting is so new that it defies generalizations. At this point the best we can do is ask questions. How much genuine news, as opposed to opinion, music or chat, can you find on podcasts? Will citizen-created podcasting reach the same level of quality as in its written forms? What percentage of podcasters have professional training or some elementary skills in creating audio? What sorts of politics has podcasting attracted? In North America and Western Europe the left seems to have jumped into the act first, but since 2007 dominant media podcasting has expanded enormously. High-level newspaper and TV journalists and even the state-controlled Voice of America have latched on to the trend. With the importance of news radio around the world, can we expect podcasting to develop a similar significance? At the moment it seems that podcasting is a form of aural news beyond the reach of the world's poorest people.[13]

Broadcast Yourself

YouTube burst into the online world in 2005, launched as a way for anyone to post video online. Its start-up costs amounted to about $11 million. To a large extent this ever-expanding site has been dominated by US youth anxious to share in the genre of TV bloopers. Others see it as a way of promoting their lifestyle and have no compunction about allowing millions into their lives — warts, tattoos and all. YouTube's motto, "broadcast yourself," suggests the two contradictory possibilities opened up to users. One emphasizes the democratic ideal that anyone can broadcast and the other encourages a largely self-centered activity.

YouTube soon became a source for news, which was quickly recognized by mainstream news agencies and their upstart Internet rivals. In 2006 Google purchased the entire operation. US news almost totally dominates on YouTube (e.g., on September 20, 2009, seven of the twelve top news clips focused on the US) but channels from China and Taiwan are growing quickly. Mixed in with the millions of clips – the ridiculous, the absurd, the mindless, the grotesque – are significant pieces of world news, often unavailable elsewhere. This includes the broadcasts of Al-Jazeera, a first for most viewers in the West, as well as the chilling documentary, *Shooting the Messenger,* on the deliberate killing and harassment of journalists in conflict zones, released in June 2008.

Politicians from Italy, France and the US have also started using the site for promoting themselves. YouTube freely mixes real news and fake news, commentary and advertising. Often the distinctions get a little murky.

YouTube has expanded the possibilities for news. For example, it has worked as a site for dissident Iranians and Tibetans to post underground images and surreptitious footage. Numerous videos, shot in the streets with cellphone cameras during the 2009 elections, show Iran's police forces harassing, assaulting and arresting women. For this reason Iran and many other countries, including

The Digital Gap

World Internet Users, 2008

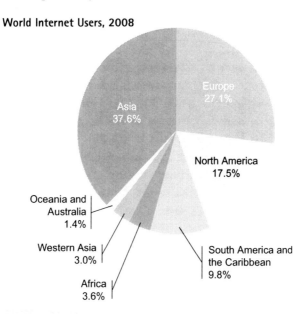

Europe
27.1%

Asia
37.6%

North America
17.5%

Oceania and
Australia
1.4%

Western Asia
3.0%

South America and
the Caribbean
9.8%

Africa
3.6%

Percentage of Households with Internet, 2008

Korea – 94%

Canada – 64%

EU / UK – 56%

US – 56%

Peru – 5%

Cameroon – 1%

Source: International Telecommunications Union, *The Global Information Society: A Statistical View* (UNESCO, 2008)

Turkey, Brazil and Thailand – as well as the US Army – have at times blocked access to the site.

Online News Trends

For every form of Internet activity, including specialized science journalism, voices from the US still dominate. This is true both in terms of numbers and the ability to shout the loudest, a pattern that follows the well-worn path of Hollywood and popular music. The blogosphere and YouTube in particular show this bias. For more conventional news sites, however, computer users are increasingly moving toward a range of sources, including Agence France-Presse, Zee TV and Al-Jazeera.

Some trends reveal big changes. According to commercial service companies and the United Nations, Asia now hosts the most Internet users (not percentage of households with Internet), followed by Europe, with North America third. Yet while Asia has the most users, the English language dominates, even in China. However, the rapid adoption of the Internet in China and India probably points to a future of decreased American influence and a proliferation of other languages online. India, in particular, because of its huge technical and engineering sectors filled with highly skilled university graduates, seems poised to be an Internet leader.

More online news sites get launched every day. Some offer real alternatives to the dominant media, but many online news, blogs and social networking services accelerate some dangerous trends. For example, they encourage immediacy, speed and first impressions as the prevailing news values. In most cases they emphasize breadth at the expense of depth of information. Many accelerate the sound-bite culture — a culture of surface phenomena and amnesia, devoid of context and history. Online news sites push the older news media, particularly twenty-four-hour TV, to follow suit. Online sites also contribute to the blurring of boundaries between news and commerce. Many influential online sites depend on advertising, a dependence that affects their news values. They set fewer rules than their old media counterparts about conflicts of interest for writers, bloggers or editors. They also have fewer mechanisms for recognizing, labeling or rejecting fake news, or even for spotting errors of fact. In the online world, news creation is the priority; news editing is not.

For the dominant media, online advertising has grown rapidly, and some predict that advertising will eventually desert the old media entirely. But in 2009 online lagged far behind print in generating revenue. Newspapers and broadcasters simply can't charge as much for online ads.

Yet even with these problems, online news shows great promise for a world of democratic media. In countries burdened with a tightly controlled media the new possibilities opened up online become particularly important. And in liberal democracies we now have the ability to select news, information and opinions from an international ocean that is both deep and wide. The fresh sources of online news allow us to embark on a surfing safari far beyond our old boundaries.

Chapter 6
Ethics

> There is more nonsense written and spoken about ethics than any other issue in journalism.
> — David Randall[1]

As a working reporter and journalism teacher, Randall ought to know. But his comment also reflects a cynicism toward ethical issues that is common in the news business. It's an attitude shared by many journalists and editors. Ethics is a barrier that gets in the way of doing their job and getting the story. Ethics, they say, preoccupies academics who lack knowledge of real-world journalism. Of course, not all newspeople share those attitudes. Many reflect constantly on their work and their methods. They question whether their articles and images treat people fairly and whether their stories might cause harm. And they know that a huge proportion of their audience holds a very low opinion of journalists and their ethics.

Ethics concerns the choices that we make about how to live, how to behave, how to treat others—choices made according to a set of general principles or in a particular situation. In going about their work, journalists face three types of ethical questions: those in relationship to their sources and the people they encounter; those in relationship to their audience of viewers, listeners and readers; and those in relationship to themselves as professionals trying to maintain a good reputation and do the job to the best of their ability.[2]

These apply equally to all stories, from a small item on lost pets for community radio to a complex investigation into police corruption for national television. As they gather news, follow stories and investigate, journalists talk with dozens of people a day. In all these interactions they face choices about how to act, how to speak, how to present themselves, how much information to divulge and how careful they should be about privacy.

After the news-gathering phase, journalists then edit or write up the story in order to communicate with their audience. Here again, each person faces numerous ethical issues. Does the story provide the audience with accurate information and enough context to understand? Or does making it a better story involve including misleading information that is impossible for the audience to detect? Each journalist has to live with her or his story and its consequences, sometimes for many years. Is it something that they can be proud of?

News media representatives also wield power. For many citizens, even in democracies, journalists can be intimidating — they seem to represent authority, often arriving on the scene with police and other officials. In addition, journalists know the consequences of speaking publicly and they know the law. This puts them at a clear advantage over most citizens. For example, if a reporter turns up at your house and starts asking questions, do you understand the consequences of being quoted on TV? Could it cause trouble for you at work? These questions are multiplied ten-fold in repressive countries. In some areas of the world just being seen with a reporter can mean arrest and serious danger. Reporters can usually leave; their sources cannot. It's one thing to pass on a rumor to a neighbor and quite another to report such a rumor on a national radio program heard by millions. This ability to cause harm is recognized in Western legal systems through the laws of libel (written harm) and slander (spoken harm).

Over the past four centuries the media have fought for and won special rights — to investigate people and even infringe on privacy in the name of a higher good; to go out into the world and demand answers; to have more access to information than ordinary citizens. This comes with the responsibility to be accurate and fair in reporting what they find. It also comes with the responsibility to be a balancing force in society — a check on government and other power centers such as the military, the church and big business.

Most news media operate in search of profit; hence a tension or outright contradiction often develops in maintaining objective, non-exploitative reporting. In these situations owners, competitors and advertisers all exert pressures that can harm news-gathering and reporting. For example, some observers maintain that General Electric's ownership of NBC News in the US has hindered or blocked stories on GE's involvement in the weapons business and the nuclear industry.[3] But operating news for profit hurts small organizations as well, especially in towns where a TV station or paper may rely heavily on one advertiser. For example, what happens when a union tries to organize the local dog food factory but the company that runs the factory has been running weekly ads in the paper for years? Will the paper cover the story?

Small-Scale Ethics

Ethical dilemmas don't simply leap out when dealing with big issues or in situations of great harm or consequences. In fact, journalists and their editors and producers make ethical decisions all the time. These can be either conscious or not. Sometimes there's an ethical dimension to the placing of a comma, the buying of a drink for a news source, the repeating of a teeny white lie. Often the reporter or producer doesn't think their action will be noticed or matter to anyone; later, that action might turn out to matter a great deal.

Writing honestly means many things. It means quoting people correctly and describing a news scene accurately. Many good journalists go with this advice, "Write only what you know to be true, don't include what you think *must* be true." Writing honestly can also present choices about style, for example, cleaning up the language. If someone speaks with bad grammar do you leave that in or make corrections? If a woman on welfare swears, is it all right to leave those words in? What if it's the mayor? These small decisions can be critical in determining how the audience will understand or interpret a story.

Many journalists present themselves as heroic investigators, risking danger in harrowing situations. They talk about "giving people a voice." Drive-by journalism implies the kind of reporting that dashes here and there and then presents itself as expertise. The ethical journalist, on the other hand, remains modest about her knowledge and knows that a quick trip out to the hinterland may only scratch the surface. Good journalists also realize that they can usually return to home and comfort, whereas their sources and subjects cannot.

News-media ethics often get compromised when reporters, editors and producers hide behind their general principles. Unfair, sloppy and biased reporting comes into being because the journalist has rationalized that it's the public's right to know. In fact, more examples of sleazy journalism take place under the excuse of this category than any other. Likewise, the journalist's credo of objectivity can often function as a cover for a lack of initiative or an unwillingness to take on powerful interests. Many other dubious practices take place because cynical reporters, who lack human feeling, can say that they are behaving according to professional neutrality.

The creation of a news story requires ethical as well as artistic choices. Some story formats, especially for

TV and radio, make it difficult to deal with complex situations. They seem to work by eliminating the gray, pushing the conflict or ignoring the context. They can also create juxtapositions or parallels that don't exist through techniques of editing picture and sound. To take a simple example, do you as a film editor insert reaction shots of people yawning or grimacing while you are filming someone making a speech?

Has the reporter talked to enough people to verify that the story is accurate and fair? Has she or he consulted a wide enough range of people, some of whom might bring different viewpoints to the story? To some extent this boils down to a reporter's energy or laziness, but not always. Sometimes reporters stick with the usual sources because they confirm their bias. It is clear that journalists should avoid taking favors (e.g., meals, trips, tickets) from their regular contacts or anyone involved in their story. That should apply to giving favors as well. This becomes more difficult in small cities, where reporters rub shoulders with other members of the community, or when working on a specialized newsbeat.

Medium-Scale Ethics

Reporters deal with many people, from the rich and powerful to the down and out. They need these people to talk (sometimes on-camera), to recount what happened, to give an opinion or to refute an accusation. Stories are nothing without people. The way that reporters relate to these people brings up many ethical choices. Although it's not generally recommended, reporters often hide their identity to put people at ease. Lots of people get nervous around reporters and others simply refuse to talk. In more complicated stories reporters sometimes work undercover in order to dig out information. The ethics of these situations depend on the seriousness of the story and whether or not innocent people are harmed by the deception.

A much more complex situation occurs when an undercover reporter gets involved in crime, or when reporters set up a sting operation, designed to trap someone into admitting to or even committing a crime. Famous cases involving reporters who infiltrate youth gangs and help plan crimes or trap potential pedophiles run the risk of tainting all journalism.

Representations of People and Groups
"Why are British newsrooms so hideously white?" asked a 2001 article in the *Independent*. This echoed a controversial statement by the BBC director-general who said that his organization was having difficulty retaining journalists from minority ethnic backgrounds.[4]

The news media reflect the biases of the organizations that own them and the people who work in them. Thus, very few media outlets in the world reflect the diversity of peoples in their societies. This applies to news content, news presenters and journalists. For example, are black people seen in a variety of stories or usually only in sports and crime? Does a reporter give the impression that an interview with one gay man represents all the views of that community? Are Iranians always shown demonstrating wildly in the street? Editors and producers in particular have an ethical duty to their audience to think about the effects of stories, not only on individuals but on social groups. This is just as important as a reporter's duty to be honest with individual people. This is more than a small-scale ethical issue that can be improved with better behavior on the part of reporters. It speaks to the stance of the news outfit as a whole.

Conflicts of Interest
The separation of editorial and advertising departments ranks high as a sacred principle in the news business. A particularly bad instance where that separation has been breached is the partnership of Germany's *Bild*, the largest circulation paper in Europe, with McDonald's restaurants. The paper regularly runs so-called news items about the chain. Other conflicts of interest crop up when the boundaries between journalists and police or government departments get too close. The decision of where to place the camera during a street demonstration should involve some thinking about neutrality versus conflict of interest. When TV news crews film from behind the police lines they create an identification with the police and a sense that the demonstrators are dangerous.

News Values
The general application of news values usually takes place among senior editors, marketing managers and owners.

Their interests and biases and the way they try to "position" or "brand" the news organization commercially and politically determine the culture for journalists. For example, many newspapers have decided that sex, drugs, sleaze and sensation sell papers. Many elevate hypocrisy to unheard-of levels by the way that they combine sleaze with great moral indignation. A quick look at Murdoch's *Sun, News of the World* and *New York Post*, Canada's *Sun* chain, Germany's *Bild* and Mexico's *La nota roja*, or "grisly pages," will give you the idea.[5] Roy Greenslade, a former newspaper editor and the author of *Press Gang,* notes that Murdoch's British tabloid, the *Sun,* "cultivated sex, yet decried sexual license in its leading articles. It lured readers to play bingo for huge prizes while lecturing them on the vice of a something-for-nothing society. It encouraged people to sell their sexual secrets while holding them up to ridicule."[6]

When a news organization considers its priorities and its approach to the news it often thinks of the balance it must strike between micro and macro issues. Another balance centers on the distinction between "public interest" and what interests the public. They're often very different. When thinking about the public interest producers might ask how much a TV station should support such things as campaigns for more substantial debate among politicians or for higher school standards. Or should the station remain a passive recorder of passing interests or whatever events come up? These are not idle questions about style or building a "brand." They are ethical questions.

Tabs and Trash

What should we make of celebrity journalism and the paparazzi? Most of their investigations focus on small-time sex, drugs and crime. They indulge in secret filming, dubious TV reconstructions, scandal-mongering and provocative editing and music. They involve us in a sensationalist downward spiral with nonsense, not only about celebrities, but about those furthest down the social ladder. They serve the law-and-order agendas of their producers. In the US, CNN's Nancy Grace, a former criminal prosecutor, provides the most obvious example of not only scandal but vengeance media. This host and her producers play reporter, prosecutor, judge and jury.

Large–Scale Ethics

News ethics don't just involve reporters making small decisions about how to gather news and how to write it up or shape it for radio, TV and the Internet. They also stem from the news culture fostered by senior management and owners of the organization. But we might look even further and consider how societies see the role of journalism and the nature of news organizations in general.

In the US style of journalism, now practiced widely around the world, news means facts and objectivity, neutrality and detachment. But in other places — France and much of South America, for example — the news remains more closely tied to opinion and journalists are much more up-front about their biases. They consider this more honest. They claim that the US approach can never be free of bias and opinion, and therefore it shouldn't pretend to be. Of course, French journalism doesn't abandon factual reporting any more than its US counterpart avoids point of view.

But these general approaches do make for different types of journalism. An ethical approach to news philosophies should remind audiences continually of these differences. Each approach has its strengths and weaknesses. Each can be carried too far. When US-style journalists claim that all they do is report the news, or simply communicate without selecting and shaping the news, they are being unethical. And when French or other newspeople claim that all news is simply opinion, they unethically abandon an important responsibility to provide their audiences with clear and accurate information about the world.

All news organizations need to decide on their priorities. Do they see themselves as accountable to the public, to government, to corporate advertisers or simply to themselves? In the news world today you can easily find news groups aligned to any of these masters. Owners such as the Asper family in Canada or Silvio Berlusconi, the prime minister and also the most powerful media owner in Italy, have chosen profits and power as the key priorities.

Other news groups choose close alliance with the government in power (or were set up for that purpose). The media of China and Iran fit this category. Still others, such as the BBC and the European "public broadcasters," pledge allegiance to the broad interests of citizens, as long as journalists don't overstep their mandate and offend their governments.

News organizations that care mostly for private profit and power seldom reflect the diversity of their societies. In the West, although some progress has been made in the employment of women journalists, the culture of reporting in the old media remains doggedly white and male. In all of the Americas most media do not reflect or engage with the indigenous peoples in their midst, who in some cases, such as in Guatemala and Peru, constitute a majority. When this situation is so clear we must conclude that newsgroups choose to maintain the status quo and feel little accountability to weaker groups, which often means oppressing or suppressing these other voices.

Some truly independent newsgroups choose to work for the public interest, even if that means distancing themselves from the political system in which they operate. Many of these groups work on a modest scale, but sometimes their influence has been great, such as in Korea, Chile and Argentina, as we'll see in the next chapter on investigative reporting.

News for Profit

When governments and corporations set up a news system based primarily on profit they have made an ethical decision. They have decided that other principles, such as diversity of opinion or universal access to information, will be less important in their societies. During the 1930s the US government opted for a profit system in radio and TV news, and in 1996 they did the same with the Internet. These were not simply mechanical or inevitable choices about politics and economics. They determine the type of society that their citizens will live in.[7]

These ethical questions are never simple. Many issues can quickly become extremely complex. We can demand, however, that our news organizations set radically different priorities, that they take their stated responsibilities seriously and that they drop the cynical attitudes that treat ethics like a dirty word. It is unlikely, of course, that capitalist big media and their repressive state versions will suddenly see the light and operate in support of democracy. But we should demand it anyway, through organizations, communities and political parties. The process will remind us that news is power. And power can be overturned.

Chapter 7
Investigative Journalism

Whenever the topic of investigative journalism crops up someone always exclaims, "Isn't all journalism investigative?" Perhaps it should be. Investigative journalists aren't satisfied to communicate the words of authorities. They seek out other opinions from people who don't have access to media. They also strive to move beyond a typical charge and counter-charge type of story. Some would say that investigative means exposing something that has been hidden — in many cases something that someone wants to keep hidden. Thus the work requires active and original reporting into wrongdoing.

There are three main investigative methods: digging, collaborating and analyzing. The Digger journalist searches more broadly and digs deeper than in regular news stories in order to uncover facts and situations previously unknown. In 2005, Louise Elliot, a Canadian radio journalist, worked to uncover the secret testing of the chemical weapons Agent Orange and Agent Purple in Canada during the 1960s.[1] The Collaborator works with insiders who have a story to tell about corporate or government problems. In South America, where this is the key practice, it's called "Watchdog Journalism." There, reporters don't have the same access to information or freedom of movement as reporters in the North. Instead they must rely much more on inside sources, who provide information, leak documents and generally foster investigations. In this way the investigation functions more as a joint effort than the exploits of a lone crusading journalist. The Analyst carefully sifts through public records, speeches and other media stories to uncover discrepancies or contradictions.[2] In many cases journalists use two or three of these methods.

The news media like to trumpet their investigative work because it builds up their image, implying that this kind of reporting defines their entire operation. In fact, investigative work remains a minority activity pursued by very few journalists. Nevertheless, it does happen — all the time, in most types of news media. And it plays a crucial role in society, a role that other groups have not played.

Tony Harcup reminds us not to romanticize this work: "Most investigative journalism would not make for dramatic footage — the meticulous cross-referencing of information strands, the days phoning people with similar names... and hours poring over obscure documents or computer databases until your eyes scream for mercy."[3] For many people in the news business investigative work represents the highest calling in the profession. That's partly because the work requires the most active kind of reporting. It's not simply responding to events as they appear on the surface of life. Although even basic reporting requires the active work of news-gathering and construction of a story, investigations require an additional and original effort to uncover information — a process that is much more difficult and often dangerous.

Not all investigative journalism practices the same methods or digs to the same degree, but all can play an important role in our societies.

Citizen and Consumer Complaints

Shoddy business practices, faulty products, misleading ads: these social and economic problems should be pregnant. In 1990, the editorial offices were attacked with a phosphorous-grenade firebomb. But the *Namibian* never missed an edition and Lister still works at the paper as an editor.

María Teresa Ronderos is the editor-in-chief of *Semana*, Colombia's leading newsmagazine. She has written many stories about her country's scandals involving drug money and about secret links between politicians and para-military groups responsible for numerous massacres and political executions.

Marites Dañguilan Vitug is a co-founder of the Philippine Center for Investigative Journalism. Vitug has reported extensively on environmental issues and has been threatened with imprisonment for her investigations into illegal logging operations.

Anna Politkovskaya, a Russian journalist, was assassinated in October 2006, likely in retaliation for her reporting of major human rights abuses by the Russian army in Chechnya. Over a twenty-year career, she traveled constantly into war zones, writing critically of President Putin as well as of Chechen militants.[5]

examined by government inspectors, business and trade associations or fraud investigators. But these groups often fail in their jobs. That's when the existence of a responsible press becomes vital. Many newspapers and local TV outlets employ a journalist to act as a consumer advocate, using a kind of David and Goliath story to help the "little guy." These reports often focus on small-time crooks or tradespeople, such as car mechanics and home builders. Usually the light of bad publicity and public shaming in the face of an aggressive reporter tips the scales to right the wrong. The TV reporter getting out there to confront the crooks head-on makes for great entertainment, especially if someone tries to clam up or avoid the reporter.

Crimes and Misdemeanors

Cases of corruption, cronyism, greed or failure to protect public health and safety should normally be handled by the police, courts or government inspectors and auditors. But the police and other officials don't always act, or they lack the expertise and the time to investigate. The unmasking of white-collar crimes requires investigations by people with specialized business or accounting skills. Investigations into these crimes also require determined reporting over a long period. The stories often get started or become successful through key evidence provided by conscientious whistle-blowers or inside sources. A compelling Hollywood film called *The Insider* (1999), starring Russell Crowe, tells the tale of a tobacco company whistleblower who worked with the journalist Lowell Bergman to reveal the illegal practices in the cigarette business. Both the insider's special knowledge and the additional work by Bergman made their story irrefutable. Other famous cases include investigations that have freed the wrongly accused or revealed dirty dealing that sent crooks to jail.

The media in many countries have, through hard digging, been able to unmask serious conflicts of interest between government and business leaders. It's probably safe to say that all Western democracies have experienced significant scandals of bribery, insider information, kickbacks and special deals. And these scandals first came to light not through the police or the courts but through journalists who had the time, the nerve and a good dose of moral outrage to ask the awkward questions.

Large-Scale Problems in the System

The problems in this category range far beyond the occasional wrongdoing. They extend to issues at the heart of a society or to the system overall – systemic problems. Such issues include the workings of government, the power of the legal system, the role of business and the military, class and caste structures, and the state of human and civil rights.

Other systemic abuse involves authoritarian states that stifle the independence of their judges or favor some groups over others. For example, in Pakistan in 2008 the military government ignored the constitution and fired all the Supreme Court judges because they disliked the judges' rulings. Reporters Without Borders states that in May 2008 Pakistani television was banned from showing live events.[6] Some governments systematically repress minority (or majority) ethnic groups, such as aboriginal communities in much of Central America. In many countries the news media occupy the best position to call attention to these problems. Unfortunately, the dominant media rarely do. When it comes to investigating large-scale structural problems the role often falls to those independent, sometimes underground groups on the margins.

All forms of serious investigative journalism require time, money and legal backup. One reason is because accused wrongdoers often retaliate by threatening lawsuits. They also hire lawyers, spin doctors and public relations firms to argue their cases and slow down the investigation. Obviously, everyone has the right to defend themselves against media accusations. But people with money can make all but the toughest news outlets back off. It also helps if the journalist receives the backing of a strong media organization – to take on some of the work, to lend credibility and to share the consequences. It's one thing when an independent and well-financed paper like *Le Monde* in France takes on a story and something else again when a reporter toils as a freelancer or works for community radio.

Investigative journalism, though generally expensive, appears in all kinds of media. In some countries or political situations even minor investigative reports never appear in the mainstream media. For example, in many South American countries, in the 1970s, military dictatorships made such reporting nearly impossible. Editors and journalists who raised questions were fired, jailed or murdered. Faced with that situation only the small, underground press could report government crimes.

In North America the news media operate almost exclusively through advertising. (Even the Public Broadcasting System in the US and the Canadian Broadcasting Corporation TV services rely on huge injections of commercial advertising money.) In addition, many of the media outlets are owned by large corporations. This makes it difficult for reporters and editors to run investigative stories on systemic business corruption and white-collar crime or to assign reporters to cover stories from the perspective of workers. For this reason most investigative reporting in North America and Western Europe focuses on individual crimes and misdemeanors stories — cases of isolated government corruption and civil or human rights abuses. Although these serious problems should be exposed, it is unfortunate when democracies are weakened because investigations have shied away from examining economic abuse and systemic injustice.

The Situation Today

Why don't we get more investigative reporting? Journalists and editors say it's actually very rare, and some media observers believe that for the dominant media the days of complex, time-consuming, expensive features have past. Not all reporters are cut out for the work. Sometimes the job requires a particular knowledge of, or sensitivity to, different cultures. Other times the task requires a toughness or aggressiveness to keep pushing reluctant witnesses or to confront wrongdoers head-on. Some reporters face more than the evasive or obstreperous people they'd like to talk to. They face real dangers.

News media owners rarely interfere directly in the running of the editorial side of operations. However, many owners make their views known, for example, about a current regime or government policy. And advertisers don't always like investigations, especially when reporters sniff around their particular business sector. Editors and reporters get the hint. In almost all countries dominant media owners rub shoulders with the elites in government and other businesses. They often act as company co-directors and belong to the same social networks.

The professional culture of journalists and newspeople, with their ideology of balance, objectivity and separation from society, puts a brake on investigations as well. Unfortunately, many journalists develop a hardened and cynical attitude to the world. Those who take up causes often get labeled naive or "earnest." In this sort of atmosphere investigative work into social problems seems a bit of an embarrassment, not fitting for an "objective" professional. Investigative journalism always runs the risk of sensationalism when reporters and editors believe they have uncovered something important. In the rush to pump out stories ahead of their rivals complex situations can become greatly oversimplified. News media also risk abusing their power when they initiate campaigns or see themselves as accountable to no one.

Nevertheless, without serious, in-depth investigations crooks, governments and corporations would get away with much more. The need for this work counts double for international news, especially during times of war.

Chapter 8
War and International News

Sahar Hussein al-Haideri, 45, a courageous Iraqi journalist, has been murdered outside her home in Mosul, the latest victim of attacks against Muslim women reporters.
— Institute for War and Peace Reporting,
June 7, 2007

The outbreak of war is newsworthy by any definition. Wars usually involve a major loss of life — of thousands, sometimes millions of people — and cause significant disruptions of economic, social and political life. During a war, governments and armies carry out horrific deeds in the name of their nation-state and its citizens. They claim to be protecting or assisting citizens in the name of democracy, human rights, nationality and religion. But there are practical and ethical reasons why we want to know what's going on in any war.

Wars and the way the dominant media handle them should concern us because in modern times more civilians get killed than soldiers. That's been the case since the Second World War and it continues today in Iraq, Sudan, Sri Lanka and the Democratic Republic of the Congo. Wars are no longer the preserve of professional soldiers fighting other armies in far-off, unpopulated spots. Today's battles take place in cities, suburbs, markets, churches, schools and neighborhoods, affecting as many children as adults. In fact, most deaths from war come not from battles at all. They come from famine and disease. These are not natural disasters, but human-made, deliberate acts of war.

News organizations should take their ethical responsibilities particularly seriously in wartime. Both the public and governments look to the media for information. Civilian governments that rely solely on their military for news seldom get the whole story. This is as true in Europe as in Pakistan. Secrecy is paramount for the military during wartime. The less that politicians and the public know the better. News of blunders, defeats or the existence of massive bombing campaigns that result in "collateral" damage seldom help the military.[1]

Media coverage can shape foreign policy as well. Government leaders often assume that if the news media has taken no interest the public doesn't care either. American media scholar Philip Seib suggests that in situations where an argument might be made for international intervention to stop a country engaged in human-rights abuses, the role of the press becomes particularly crucial.[2] He argues that for Somalia, Rwanda, Sierra Leone, East Timor and Bosnia, in the 1990s, better media coverage of impending disasters might have prompted a more timely and humane response from the world's powerful countries. The same holds for the Iran-Iraq war of the 1980s, of which the Western media took little notice. How different the world situation might be today if we had learned during those years that the US was actively supporting Saddam Hussein's Iraq.

Seib's pessimistic conclusion is that most media coverage of international conflicts comes only once the shooting begins. The result is sensational but superficial coverage, which lasts only until the most dramatic events have past. Phillip Knightley, author of *The First Casualty*, the definitive history of media and war, agrees.[3] Media coverage of war, particularly for television, he says, emphasizes dramatic pictures of "our soldiers." When that's not possible, as in the case of the US withdrawal of ground troops from Vietnam after 1973 and from Somalia in the 1990s, the media lost interest. And today? "In Canada, for instance, says journalist David McKie, the deaths of Canadian soldiers [in Afghanistan] have become old news."[4]

Not all wars are alike, of course. For a start there are our wars and other people's wars. Our wars involve our government and military fighting (or peacekeeping) in our name. In the other wars we don't seem to be involved. However, in today's connected globe it turns out that we do have connections with most other governments and their citizens. We might, for example, be trading partners or linked by political alliances, such as the British Commonwealth. And a large proportion of our citizens have strong family ties to another country of origin.

Our Wars

Most honest journalists would admit that the reporting of past wars where "we" were directly involved has been very poor. Knightley's extensive research shows that the reporting was "bad, biased, censored, timid and incompetent, involving willful fabrications and self-censorship."[5] Why has this been so? What hurdles stand in the way of good coverage when "our" military joins the battle?

Pure and simple censorship sets the tone, managed by senior levels of government, the people who decide "we" should go to war, and the military, those given the task of winning. In addition, media owners, editors and journalists, despite their professional oaths to report without bias, somewhat naturally fall into patriotic self-censorship. Because of this journalists are loath to file stories that might hurt morale or in the old phrase, "give comfort to the enemy." Writing positive stories shows that you're "onside," that you understand the hardships and dangers facing ordinary soldiers. To be critical hurts military recruitment and translates into lack of support for "our boys," who are off risking their necks for us.

Journalists themselves often develop ways of behaving that impede accurate and balanced coverage. Macho involvement of the kind epitomized by writer Ernest Hemingway, who reveled in his own fighting involvement, takes on a guts-and-glory framework – the "war is hell, but it's manly" syndrome. This sort of war-is-cool approach is still alive and celebrated. Witness the Canadian reporter Arthur Kent, who during the 1991 Gulf War became known as the "Scud Stud."[6] TV reporters in particular can come to believe that the only "story" is the most violently dramatic one. This makes for a very narrow definition of news.

Without a doubt war correspondents face enormously difficult and dangerous conditions. Even those who operate with the military's blessing run tremendous risks. In today's conflicts few combatants respect the "gentlemen's" rules that in the past might have granted the press some safety. Many of the world's most vicious conflicts have not even been declared wars; rather, each side views the other as terrorists, criminals or enemy combatants. In addition, very young fighters often receive little or no training. Routine mistakes and freelance killings are common. In the worst cases, many of the combatants are intoxicated or drugged, so the niceties of international law or respect for the rights of journalists hardly matter. In the early days of the Iraq War, US bombers hit the Al-Jazeera TV station, killing a cameraman, and the insurgents continue to kidnap and kill reporters of all stripes. US planes also bombed the Al-Jazeera offices in Kabul, Afghanistan, in 2001.[7]

Even mainstream journalists who in general support their country's war but who write critical articles about the conduct of the war get branded as traitors. David

Most journalists who are killed are not famous. They are local people, many working for foreign companies when they die. So why do they do it? In Iraq, where sixty-five journalists were killed in 2007, almost a third of the total, many explain their motivation in powerful terms: reporting the disaster that has befallen their country is a patriotic vocation.[8]

Many women journalists have been killed in Iraq, Afghanistan, Uzbekistan and other Islamic countries. This may relate to the hostility on the part of some extremists to women working in the public sphere.

Halberstam and Peter Arnett were two such reporters. During the Vietnam War, Halberstam, senior correspondent for the *New York Times,* wrote truthfully about the strength of the communist Vietcong army. For this President Kennedy tried to force the *Times* to have him replaced.[9] In 2003, conservative US senators called for the New Zealand-born reporter Peter Arnett to be tried for treason. He had given an interview to Iraqi TV saying that the US military strategy had failed and the war would not be won quickly. Arnett's long-time employers at NBC and the *National Geographic* immediately dumped him.

Wilfred Burchett, a more radical journalist, faced the same treatment. Burchett, an Australian communist, was the first journalist to report on the radiation effects of the atomic bomb in Hiroshima. Until then the US military had denied any such effects. Burchett went on to cover the Vietnam War from Hanoi. There he witnessed, often from underground shelters, the effects of the US bombing raids.

Their Wars

In the other type of war — their war — we don't seem to be involved and the combatants pose no danger to us. Their wars rarely fit our standard news patterns. In these cases the overt bias due to patriotism of media people should present less of a barrier to decent reporting. But there are other hurdles to well-informed coverage. No one should doubt the dangers involved in covering a war when the journalist has no military backup. Journalists often face rugged mountain and jungle terrain littered with landmines and certainly no hotels, and often no easy food source. It could be that both sides are hostile to outsiders, including UN peacekeeping troops. Many journalists have been badly injured, killed or kidnapped in serious conflicts since the year 2000.

However, in the coverage of "their wars" the biggest problem is ignorance. When so many of our notions about wartime conflict come from films, TV shows, even comics, do we have the tools to understand? If we have no troops involved, what's the incentive to become better informed about the parties in conflict? For example, no major Western newsgroups, with the occasional exception of the BBC, employ regular correspondents anywhere in Africa.

In addition to ignorance and the difficulty of fitting

their wars into standard war reporting conventions, other forms of censorship come into play. Most editors and journalists don't trust reporters who work for unfamiliar newsgroups. The larger and more mainstream the news organization, the less it trusts others with the news. For example, during the ongoing conflicts in Pakistan, Western news organizations send their own people and rely exclusively on their reports. We rarely hear analysis from Pakistani journalists. Ironically then, we get reports from people who fly in for a short visit rather than from people who have lived there all their lives. In fact, Western newspeople usually rely heavily on local journalists for contacts, logistics and safety. They just don't want to broadcast their opinions.

Philip Seib's study of the US media and its relation to foreign policy leads him to the conclusion that many of the problems, confusions and failures stem from pure and simple racism.[10] This takes several forms. First, it's a reflection of the demographic make-up of most newsrooms. White men still rule the show. Second, big media often perceive wars in Africa, Asia and South America as having been born in ancient racial conflicts. Too many news reports start and finish with the sense that nothing can be done because the conflicts simply run too deep.

"The implicit message at the root of that attitude," says Seib, is that "'These are savages, not worth much of our attention, and certainly not our intervention.'"

This is where laziness and racism blend together smoothly. Serious reporting would look into recent history and dig for current economic and political injustices. But this presents a much more difficult challenge. It also requires educating Western audiences about the complexities of the world.

Types of War Coverage

War reporting can take many forms. Some writers take the gung-ho for "our side" approach ("We're right and our soldiers are heroes"). Some attempt to be partisan but sober ("We're right but war is a dirty business"). Some become critical but not anti-war ("We shouldn't be in this particular mess"). Some take up an anti-war approach ("We should not be fighting, at least not in this war"). And a few rare journalists position themselves to report from a radically distinct vantage point, the "other side."

Reporters need to develop a relationship with the military. This determines how they get access to soldiers and battle zones. Some manage to work independently with no travel restrictions. Others work in a group or pool, and tend to be guided by military escorts. This is generally the way the military likes it. A third group, called embedded, travel individually with a small group of soldiers, hardly a recipe for objectivity. In Canada, many journalists heading to Afghanistan enroll in the Canadian Forces' Military Journalism course, a heady mix of safety tips and government ideology about "The Mission."

Another major distinction is whether the reporter focuses on soldiers and battles or whether she or he looks at the human costs for either the soldiers or the civilians.

Johan Galtung of Oslo, Norway, a leading scholar of international journalism, makes a passionate argument for news organizations to combine war reporting with peace journalism.[11] By analogy, he says, wouldn't it be strange if the media only talked about disease and never about health and medicine? For Galtung, peace journalism asks very different questions, such as, what is the conflict about? Who are the parties involved? What are the deeper roots of the conflict? Who is working to prevent violence? Who initiates reconstruction, reconciliation and resolution, and who is reaping benefits like reconstruction contracts?

International Reporting

Not all international news and events involve wars. Unfortunately, with the exception of natural disasters, such as the devastating tsunami that hit South and East Asia in 2006, or the earthquakes that struck China in 2008, the mainstream media of most countries do a poor job of informing their citizens about others around the world. In fact, international coverage has declined rapidly in the Western media. A British study in 2001 found that only 3 percent of British TV dealt with what they termed the "majority of humanity" in the Global South.[12] The authors call this media representation a "disaster in the era of globalization." Their reports show that "the space for in-depth factual programs examining the lives, experiences, politics and environment of the majority of the world's people — and allowing them to

Four Famous War Correspondents

William Howard Russell (1820–1907), the first modern war correspondent, reported on the Crimean War, between Britain, Russia and others (1854–1856), for the *Times* (London). Russell wrote truthful news about military failures, disease and appalling hospital conditions. The military had no real censorship in place so his reports reached a wide audience.

Kit Coleman (1864–1915), a Canadian, became the first accredited Western war correspondent. She wrote widely influential articles from Cuba on the Spanish-American War of 1898. Glorifying the conflict did not interest her. She wrote instead about the war's cruel impact on civilians.

Morgan Philips Price (1885–1973) reported accurately on the Russian Revolution for the *Manchester Guardian*. He was nearly tried for treason by the British government because he criticized the Allies' attempts to overthrow the revolutionary Bolsheviks in 1919.

Joris Ivens (1898–1989), of the Netherlands, was one of the world's most active and influential documentary filmmakers. His works on Spain, China, Indonesia, Cuba and Vietnam delivered news ignored and suppressed by dominant newspapers and radio stations. Nevertheless, his films reached huge audiences worldwide through special theater screenings.

speak for themselves without mediation — has almost totally died out." I believe that the same can be said for all the dominant Western media.

The lack of international news has serious consequences. It allows governments to act internationally with little democratic debate. It fails to inform governments about international trends, experiences and situations. It encourages citizens to believe that they are alone in the world, and thus increases the arrogance of rich countries and increases the isolation and despair of poor countries. It deprives citizens of the opportunity to explore alternative cultural experiences and practices, and it fosters racial and ethnic stereotyping.

Viewers with ties to other countries, especially first- and second-generation immigrants, feel that lack acutely. "My children were born in [Britain] and don't know anything directly of Africa. What they see of black people on TV forms a bad picture in their head about the country where I was born," says an African-born participant in a Manchester, England, media study.[13] In response, many people of ethnic and racial minorities turn to more focused news, such as Zee, from India, and Geo, from Pakistan — produced in the home country for consumption across the world.

The Future
Looking back into history we know that the need and desire for news has been with us for a long time. That need is greater today than ever. For democratic societies

serious journalism and news analysis are absolute require-
ments. It is usually only through the mass media that citizens in complex mass societies can get information about
political, social and economic issues. Even most authoritarian countries need a population that is better educated
and more flexible than in the past — it's a requirement of
globalization. And for now, newspapers still carry out the
lion's share of reporting. All other news outlets depend
on newspapers.

The current troubles facing newspaper companies,
particularly in the US, thus affect not only the news business sector but the operations of the state itself. In fact,
a collapse of the news business in the US would prove
more calamitous than a collapse of the auto industry.

Within the media business specifically, corporations
such as NBC, News Corp. and CanWest need their news
divisions to provide legitimacy for all their operations.
In the US, Canada and Britain the TV networks retain
their licenses in return for offering a news service. And
for newspapers everywhere it's the news itself that delivers an audience to advertisers.

Even as many parts of the world move further into the
online, digital universe, news delivered orally — by radio or
other forms of audio, such as mobile devices — remains the
key medium for most people in the world. This is true especially of the world's poorest. But even the simplest portable
phone requires a vast international system of satellites and
technical infrastructure. The 2008 economic crisis and sub-
sequent recession has put the brakes on these developments,

and the catastrophic problems in food prices and distribution for a billion of the world's poor will undoubtedly widen the digital gap even further. Consequently, basic radio will continue well into the future to be the medium through which most people get their news.

For its proponents, the Internet and other forms of online communication represent the future. In fact, these new forms have already changed our definitions and expectations of news. Most of us now assume that the news should be both broader and quicker than twenty years ago. We expect to have access to news sources from a wide array of places and points of view, not just be fed the old official voices of the metropolis.

We also tend to define the news as something more immediate than we did in the past. We think of news not so much as events that occurred yesterday but as something unfolding before our eyes and ears — the breaking event on the "live eye," or the direct feed to our laptop, or the cryptic text from on the spot. Corporate media pushes us to consume its news products ever faster, gulping them down without much thought: shorter, bite-sized stories pumped out without fact-checking or much editing; stories whipped off by journalists multi-tasking on video, audio and text.

Globally, the near future will see big shifts in news flows as China, India and the Arab world gain media power. Already there are more people online in Asia than anywhere else, and the commercial media operations of East, South and West Asia, exemplified by Al-Jazeera, are rapidly gaining clout beyond their traditional borders.

The Internet provides some hope for expanding international news coverage because of the astonishing array of information that now appears online. Such an international reach of the new media allows the possibility of better-informed citizens. For example, many citizens of Mexico are encouraged to know that some of the world's media have reported the widespread human rights abuses in the states of Oaxaca and Chiapas. Concerned US citizens who read international papers and websites know that their government's imperial policies just don't wash with millions of others around the world.

This utopia of information should be treated with caution, however. If, for example, you choose Google News to provide your news filter, you will find its international coverage favors US sources, with only a smattering of others. In other words the information looks broader and more international than it really is. In March 2007, a suicide bombing in Baghdad leading to twenty-eight deaths prompted Google News to say that they had collected 1,095 articles on the subject. On a closer look it became obvious that there were only two sources for these stories, one from the Associated Press and one from Reuters. All the other sources simply reworded these initial reports. And for all its international potential the Western media has become so involved with the capitalist crisis that global coverage has dropped even further. In our search for the global village of truly international news we face a grueling road ahead.

News Timeline

40,000 BC The first humans need crucial information about their surroundings. What's over the next hill? Where can we find water? Did our relatives survive the trek over the mountains? Has the hunting party found anything to eat? Right from the start, this information, or news, mixes the essential and the sensational, the important and the trivial.

59 BC Julius Caesar of Rome orders the creation of the *Acta Diurna*—the daily writing of important proclamations and official news on large white boards in busy streets. The daily public records also include births, deaths and marriages.

1042 Chinese inventors and, in 1392, Korean inventors develop printing onto paper. Unfortunately, print is controlled by a tiny minority within the powerful ruling elites.

1100 to 1400 Arab ideas and scientific learning flood into Europe. The definition of news broadens considerably due to the great need for reliable information on international activities involving trade, prices, politics, wars and science.

1447 Johannes Gutenberg, in what is now Germany, develops a printing press, based partly on a wine press. This greatly speeds the production of all written and illustrative material. The invention gets snapped up by Catholic and Protestant churches, by people writing political essays and by commercial printers for advertising and pornography. (It takes another 200 years before the widespread use of printed newspapers.)

1556 Handwritten newspapers make their first appearance. For example, a monthly *Gazetta*, named after the small coin used in Venice, publishes official notices.

1605–1690 Typeset printed newspapers serve the needs of international traders and a rising business class. The newspapers include *Le Relation* (Strasbourg, Germany/France), *Corante*, (The Netherlands and London), the *Gazette* (Paris) and *Publick Occurrences* (Boston).

1790s During the French Revolution the press starts to define itself as the Fourth Estate, an essential institution of power. News for male citizens (not slaves, aboriginals or women) now becomes a human right.

1700–1900 The idea of news narrows. The news becomes a capitalist commodity, something fresh, like vegetables, to be bought and sold. News begins to be defined solely as crucial information about recent events.

1830s The modern daily newspaper charges into the world, featuring reports and commentary on many different types of events. High-quality papers such as the *Times* (London) jostle for attention along with penny crime and sensation papers, such as the *New York Sun*.

1844 Invention of the telegraph greatly speeds up the gathering of news. It also shapes the writing of news because the telegraph companies charge by the word, so the shorter the report, the better. Flowery language is out.

1890s Commercial advertising, rather than newspaper sales, takes over as the primary means of funding newspapers. Only those papers that can attract wealthy advertisers survive.

1896 The mass paper bursts onto the scene, based on profitable advertising, a low copy price and thus a huge readership. The owner of London's *Daily Mail* and tabloid-size *Daily Mirror* (1903) says, "We've struck a goldmine."

1900   Professional, Western-style journalism, which separates "news" from "opinion" and promotes a practice of objectivity, comes to dominate in the US. Journalists hold a monopoly on news-gathering and reporting.

Small black-and-white photographs begin to appear in newspapers. Papers generally contain a huge mass of text, broken up with little white space, photos or illustrations of any kind. Gradually, as reproduction and printing technologies improve, and as ideas about what is appropriate as news broadens, photos become more prominent.

1908   Pathé-Frères film company of France introduces a five-minute weekly news program to theaters worldwide. From the 1920s to the 1950s millions get their news in this form.

1922   BBC launches the first radio news programming, expanding the scope of radio, which since its birth in 1906 had been used only for shipping communications and by amateurs.

1923   Radio Ceylon begins the first radio news in Asia.

1950s and 1960s   Television launches news broadcasts. The major US networks set up large news operations. TV's fascination with startling images pushes news analysis (then common in radio) to the sidelines. TV systems are established worldwide, set up primarily on a national basis, including in many newly independent states of Africa and Asia. TV becomes a powerful vehicle of government-controlled news in many countries.

1960   Sony's pocket-size transistor radio brings news to millions around the world, including the poor.

1980s   Twenty-four-hour news formats in radio and TV, especially Ted Turner's CNN, force a speed-up of the news cycle and a vogue for on-the-spot coverage.

2000   The Internet creates its own forms of gathering and

reporting news. Companies such as Google News, Baidu of China and hundreds of others develop huge audiences, a challenge to dominant news providers everywhere, both commercial and government.

2008–2010 Following the capitalist economic meltdown, centered in the US, many analysts believe that newspapers are doomed. They point to the failures of several famous US companies, some very old, which have disappeared or switched entirely to the online universe. The main culprit seems to be a serious decline in advertising revenue, thus resulting in much lower profit margins. Others believe that citizens no longer have the time or the desire to stay in touch with the world through a newspaper.

But these beliefs show starkly how generalizations based on the US often have no application elsewhere. In countries as diverse as Germany, India and Japan new papers continue to appear and readership, especially in India, continues its rapid growth. Many believe that the newspaper crisis in North America stems largely from the bad decisions made by the conglomerate corporations that own them. Most studies show that readers and TV viewers have not abandoned the old media for the Internet. Rather, their owners have recklessly invested in risky non-media ventures, funded by dubious financial schemes. This has led them to abandon the strengths of news journalism and produce ever-declining papers. News media companies can still make healthy profits if their owners believe in their "product," adapt to a more competitive world and allow serious journalists to do their essential work.[1]

From the beginning to today oral and pictorial communication of news has never been abandoned. Learning about the news through reading, rather than orally or through images, remains a minority practice.

Notes

1 News Is Power

1. Quoted in John Pilger, *Heroes* (London: Jonathan Cape, 1986). See also Caroline Moorehead, *Gellhorn: A Twentieth Century Life* (New York: Henry Holt, 2003).
2. The United Nations considers access to the news a basic human and civil right. See in particular Article 19 of the Universal Declaration of Human Rights, 1948, and Article 15 of the International Covenant on Economic, Social and Cultural Rights, 1966.
3. *Who Makes the News? The Global Media Monitoring Project* (WACC, 2006). See also *Women Make the News* (UNESCO, 2008) for another international perspective.
4. *National Post*, Vol. 9, No. 271, September 15, 2007.
5. Quoted in Aiden S. Enns, "Questioning Our Images of Islam," *Thunderbird, UBC Journalism Review*, Vol. 4, No. 3 (March 2002), www.journalism.ubc.ca.

2 Anatomy of the News

1. For one such study see Jon Whiten, "TV's Low-Cal Campaign Coverage: How 385 stories can tell you next to nothing about whom to vote for," *Extra!*, May/June 2008.
2. Quoted in Tony Harcup, *The Ethical Journalist* (London: Sage, 2004).
3. Tony Harcup, *Journalism: Principles and Practice* (London: Sage, 2004).
4. Daya Kishan Thussu and Des Freeman, editors, *War and the Media* (London: Sage, 2004), 123.
5. Davis Merrit, *Public Journalism and Public Life*. Second edition (Mahwah, New Jersey: Lawrence Erlbaum, 1998).
6. Paddy Scannell and David Cardiff, *A Social History of British Broadcasting*, Volume I (London: Blackwell, 1991), 118.

7. For one view of the story see BBC News, October 12, 2001, http://news.bbc.co.uk/2/hi/uk_news/politics/2013184.stm.

8. David Randall, *The Universal Journalist* (London: Pluto, 2000), 49.

9. Stuart Ewan, *PR! A Social History of Spin* (New York: Basic Books, 1998).

10. Daniel Boorstin, *The Image: A Guide to Pseudo-Events in America* (New York: Vintage, 1961).

11. Harry Glasbeek, *Wealth by Stealth: Corporate Law, Corporate Crime and the Perversion of Democracy* (Toronto: Between the Lines, 2004).

12. Project Censored demonstrates that many serious world issues get scant attention in the news, www.projectcensored.org.

13. Juan Antonio Giner, www.innovationsinnewspapers.com. April 7, 2007.

14. See, for example, Lyombe Eko, "Africa: Life in the Margins of Globalization," in Lee Artz and Yaha Kamalipour, editors, *The Media Globe: Trends in International Mass Media* (Lanham, Maryland: Rowman and Littlefield, 2007).

3 The Dominant Media

1. Quoted in *Variety*, May 15, 2007.

2. All currency is in US dollars.

3. On the *Los Angeles Times* situation see, for example, Jon Fine, "No Slick Way Out For Tribune," *Business Week*, October 9, 2006. In December 2008 the Tribune Company, parent of the *Los Angeles Times*, declared bankruptcy, claiming $13 billion in debts. What is not clear is whether it was caused by financial troubles at the newspaper or by the way the finances of the parent company were set up or by the general recession. See also Richard Siklos, "A mind-boggling deal, a company's collapse, Sam Zell's judgment day," in the *Globe and Mail*, December 12, 2008.

4. Iain Bruce, "Venezuela sets up 'CNN rival,'" BBC News, June 28, 2005.
5. All statistics are taken from *The Global Information Society: A Statistical View* (UNESCO, 2007).
6. All statistics from broadcasters' audited statements available online.
7. "Africa, Life in the Margins of Globalization" in *The Media Globe*, 12-14.
8. See Rick Rockwell and Noreene Janus, "The Triumph of the Media Elite in Postwar Central America," in Elizabeth Fox, editor, *Latin Politics, Global Media* (Austin: University of Texas Press, 2002).

4 Print, Radio and Television

1. The World Association of Newspapers, *World Press Trends, 2007*, www.wan-press.org/worldpresstrends.
2. Ibid.
3. Juan Antonio Giner, www.innovationsinnewspapers.com, March 29, 2008.
4. See Marshall Soules, http://records.viu.ca/~soules/media301/ and Fred Fedler, editor, *Reporting for the Media*, Seventh edition (New York: Oxford University Press, 2004).
5. James Agee, *A Way of Seeing: The Photographs of Helen Levitt* (New York: Viking, 1965).
6. *The Canadian Press Stylebook*, (Toronto: Canadian Press, 1999).
7. See Anne Hoy, *Photojournalism* (New York: National Geographic, 2005).
8. Robb Montgomery, Presentation, 12th World Editors Forum, Seoul, Korea, May 31, 2005.
9. School of Journalism and Mass Communications, San José State University. Grade the News, www.gradethenews.org.
10. Farm Radio International, www.farmradio.org.
11. Lyombe Eko, "Africa, Life in the Margins of Globalization," in *The Media Globe*, 7.

12. On the increasing corporate reliance at PBS, see David Barsamian, *The Decline and Fall of Public Broadcasting* (Boston: South End Press, 2002).

13. Owen Gibson, "TV news 'a turn-off for young and ethnic minorities,'" *Guardian*, July 5, 2007.

14. For the US history see Eric Barnouw, *Tube of Plenty: The Evolution of American Television*, Second edition (New York: Oxford University Press, 1990).

15. The term Fourth Estate originated in the French Revolution, where the press hoped to take its place alongside the existing Estates of nobles, clergy and commoners.

16. A recent study by Britain's Ofcom, the broadcasting regulator, reported "firm evidence of disengagement from mainstream news sources by some sectors of the young..." For a summary see Owen Gibson, "TV news 'a turn-off for young and ethnic minorities.'" *Guardian*, July 5, 2007.

17. David Westin quoted in Ken Auletta, "The Dawn Patrol: The curious rise of morning television, and the future of network news," *New Yorker*, August 8, 2005.

5 The Internet

1. Joan Connell, "Weblog Central Explained," MSNBC, March 30, 2003.

2. McLuhan discusses his concept of the Global Village in *Understanding Media* (Toronto: McGraw-Hill, 1964).

3. The Pew Research Center has developed an excellent way of evaluating web-based news sites. See "The State of the News Media: An Annual Report on American Journalism," www.journalism.org, 2008.

4. Becky Hogge, *Open Democracy*, May 5, 2007, www.opendemocracy.net.

5. UNESCO, *Global Reach, Global Internet Statistics* (2003).

6. David Barboza, *New York Times*, September 17, 2006.

7. Roy Greenslade blog, *Guardian Unlimited*, Nov. 23, 2005.

8. Salam Pax, *The Baghdad Blog* (London: Guardian Books, 2003).

9. See Katrina vanden Heuvel, "Bloggers of Iran," The Nation online, www.thenation.com/blogs, 2005 [May 23, 2007].

10. RezBiz, *My Other Fellow* blog, December 24, 2005.

11. Caroline Gluck, Interview with Oh Yeon-ho, BBC News, April 17, 2007.

12. For a lively example of citizen-created news in Brazil, see Ana Maria Brambilla, OhmyNews International, March 18, 2007.

13. A good example of a US podcast is *Radio Nation* hosted by Laura Flanders of *The Nation* magazine, www.thenation. com/section/podcasts. A good source for African news is *Pambazuka News Podcasts*, www.pambazuka.org/en/about.php. And from Canada, rabble.ca hosts *Pulse*, produced by Silence Genti, www.rabble.ca.

6 Ethics

1. David Randall, *The Universal Journalist* (London: Pluto, 2000).

2. I take this three-part approach to ethics from Jay Ruby, "The Ethics of Imagemaking," in Alan Rosenthal, editor, *New Challenges for Documentary* (Berkeley: University of California Press, 1988), 308-318.

3. See Ben Bagdikian, *The New Media Monopoly* (Boston: Beacon Press, 2004).

4. See Valerie Alia and Simone Bull, *Media and Ethnic Minorities* (University of Edinburgh Press, 2005), 10.

5. For a survey of daily front pages, see www.newsmuseum.org.

6. Roy Greenslade, *Press Gang: How Newspapers Make Profits from Propaganda* (London: Macmillan, 2003), 338.

7. See Robert McChesney, *Rich Media, Poor Democracy: Communication Politics in Dubious Times* (New York: The New Press, 1999).

7 Investigative Journalism

1. Louise Elliot, "2005 Award Winners," Canadian Association of Journalists website, www.caj.ca/mediamag/awards2006.
2. For instance, see Fredrich Engels' *The Condition of the Working-Class in England*, 1844; *I.F. Stone's Weekly* in the US in the 1950s and 1960s; and some of Noam Chomsky's writings today.
3. Tony Harcup, *Journalism: Principles and Practice* (London: Sage, 2004), 74.
4. "Member Biographies," International Consortium of Investigative Journalists, www.publicintegrity.org.
5. See also Terry Gould, *Murder Without Borders* (Toronto: Random House, 2009).
6. Reporters Without Borders, Annual Country Reports, 2008, www.rsf.org.

8 War and International News

1 See Seymour Hersh for the Bush administration's handling of this in "The Redirection," *New Yorker*, March 5, 2007.
2. Philip Seib, *Global Journalism: News and Conscience in a World of Conflict* (Lanham, Maryland: Rowman and Littlefield, 2002).
3. Phillip Knightley, *The First Casualty: The War Correspondent as Hero and Myth-Maker from the Crimea to Iraq* (Baltimore: Johns Hopkins, 2004).
4. David McKie, "Getting beyond the death watch," *Media*, Winter 2007.
5. Knightley, *The First Casualty*.
6. For stories on contemporary women war correspondents see Barbara Kopple and Bob Eisenhardt's, *Bearing Witness* (Cabin Creek Films, 2005).
7. This directly contravened the 1949 Geneva Conventions. See Maria Trombly, *Journalists' Guide to the Geneva Conventions*, Society of Professional Journalists, www.spj.org/gc.asp. See also the International Federation of Journalists, www.ifj.org.

8. David Lyn, "Local Heroes: Risk-taking in Iraq," *British Journalism Review*, Vol. 18, no. 2 (2007). See also the TV documentary *Shooting the Messenger*, which reveals the deliberate killing of journalists (produced for Al-Jazeera English by Michael Nicholson, June 17, 2008).

9. David Halberstam, "Tribute to Peter Arnett," *Columbia Journalism Review*, Nov./Dec. 2006.

10. Philip Seib, *Global Journalist*, 76.

11. Johan Galtung, "What is Peace Journalism?" www.crnetwork.ca/programs/PeaceJournalism. See also the London-based Institute for War and Peace Reporting, www.iwpr.net.

12. The Third World and Environmental Broadcasting Project, www.epolitix.com/forum/3WE.

13. Quoted in Karen Ross, "In whose image? TV criticism and Black minority viewers," in Simon Cottle, ed., *Ethnic Minorities and the Media* (London: Open University, 2000).

News Timeline

1. Two useful, Anglo-American mainstream histories are Mitchell Stephens, *History of News*, Third edition (Oxford: Oxford University Press, 2007) and Andrew Smith, *The Newspaper: An International Study* (London: Thames and Hudson, 1979). For a deeper analysis, see Brian Winston, *Messages* (London: Routledge, 2005) and James Curran and Jean Seaton, *Power without Responsibility*, Seventh edition (London: Routledge, 2009).

For Further Information

Bagdikian, Ben. *The New Media Monopoly*. Boston: Beacon Press, 2004.

Chomsky, Noam and Edward S. Herman. *Manufacturing Consent: The Political Economy of the Mass Media*. New York: Pantheon Books, 2002.

Curran, James and Jean Seaton. *Power Without Responsibility*. Seventh edition. London: Routledge, 2009.

Gould, Terry. *Murder Without Borders*. Toronto: Random House, 2009.

Harcup, Tony. *Journalism: Principles and Practice*. London: Sage, 2004.

Knightley, Phillip. *The First Casualty: The War Correspondent as Hero and Mythmaker from the Crimea to Iraq*. Baltimore: Johns Hopkins Press, 2004.

Kovach, Bill and Tom Rosenthiel. *The Elements of Journalism*. New York: Three Rivers Press, 2007.

McChesney, Robert. *Rich Media, Poor Democracy: Communication Politics in Dubious Times*. New York: The New Press, 1999.

Mosco, Vincent. *The Political Economy of Communication*. Second edition. New York: Sage, 2009.

Pilger, John. *Tell Me No Lies: Investigative Journalism and Its Triumphs*. London: Jonathan Cape, 2004.

Randall, David. *The Universal Journalist*. London: Pluto, 2000.

Waisbord, Silvio. *Watchdog Journalism in South America*. New York: Columbia University Press, 2000.

Winston, Brian. *Messages: Free Expression, Media and the West from Gutenberg to Google*. London: Routledge, 2005.

Acknowledgments

I thank Patsy Aldana and Jane Springer for their superb editing skills and everyone at Groundwood for their encouragement and support in writing this book. Thanks also to Richard Swift for his assistance in understanding journalism and world events and to Michael Jackal for his vast knowledge of newspapers and the world of publishing. My discussion of television has benefited immensely from the scholarly work of Jeremy Butler at the University of Alabama and Blaine Allan at Queen's University in Kingston, Canada. My discussion of media technology would not be possible without the historical work of Brian Winston; my understanding of journalism and war is indebted to the powerful analysis of Phillip Knightley; and my approach to the dominant media would not be possible without the many books and films of John Pilger.

As always I thank my partner, Geri Sadoway, for her support and her expertise about how the reporting of world events affects refugees and displaced peoples everywhere.

Index

CPSIA information can be obtained at www.ICGtesting.com
Printed in the USA
LVOW07s1141211014

409776LV00005B/22/P